Dear Peter,

So much gratitude
for your contribution
and support.

With love,

Ken.

UNLOCK
POTENTIAL-WITH
Love

Ken G Cooper

authorHOUSE®

AuthorHouse™ UK
1663 Liberty Drive
Bloomington, IN 47403 USA
www.authorhouse.co.uk
Phone: 0800.197.4150

Published by AuthorHouse 07/11/2017

ISBN: 978-1-5246-8067-1 (sc)
ISBN: 978-1-5246-8068-8 (e)

CONTENTS

Introducing Ken G Cooper

I am very pleased to introduce Ken and this rather special book.

There are many, many management, life coaching and self help books on the market. The fair question is whether there is room or need for one more.

Before considering this, there is also the shocking use of one of the simplest and yet so powerful four letter words, love.

Then to cap it all, there is this culture throughout the book of Christianity and the Bible. As a 'doubting Thomas' I approached these issues with a degree of scepticism and caution. Surely this is too much a private, personal belief to be used in such a public way. I can assure you that it isn't.

Ken and I met in Cornwall by chance, found many things in common, especially a shared passion for helping people through training and support. We have both seen the real strengths, qualities and skills lying undiscovered, unused and so often unrealised in the people around us. So the theme of 'unlocking potential' is completely right.

Just stopping to help, say a kind word, praise first and see the good are all traits that Ken and I have tried to use throughout our working lives. So even this has a 'Christian' or religious flavour.

It is not about conversion, preaching or indoctrination; it is merely using some stories and practices from this pretty special book.

It is about who Ken is and how he lives and has lived his life, what he has sought and found. It is based on real life experience from his work and especially from his 'unlocking potential' seminars.

He is not asking people to change their identity, their personalities, who they are. He is simply asking you to look inside yourself and use what you have.

It is quite usual that many people need help to recognise and understand the latent potential within them before looking at how they might be developed.

Ken's book is a way to help unlock this potential.

Love is the key.

Wanting to help and being willing to help, looking to see the good, praise, encouragement and recognition produces so much more.

So, yes, there is room for such a book. A simple message but one not quite used before. It is a treasure chest. One can dip in and out of it and enjoy the valuable gems of insight and experience.

Ken uses the Bible as a motivational tool. There is an honest and clear approach, and while there are several references to the Bible, isn't this knowingly, or unwittingly, the source of many stock phrases in modern management? Perhaps the most obvious and relevant to this book being "seek and ye shall find".

The Eight Core Qualities and the Guarantee of Success sections provide a guide and a direction for work and personal culture – 'it's the way to do things'. Love is very much the key.

'Happy is the man who finds wisdom'. Ken has found, enjoyed and given of his wisdom and experience and sets it out in this very useful and valuable book.

Ken's writing will help you find yourself, get to know yourself better and through development of your potential help make life richer and more rewarding.

I recommend it to you.

Peter Thomas
Consultant and business advisor, former CEO of the BII, Course Director in Multi-unit Leadership, Birmingham University Business School.

WHY READ THIS BOOK?

How often do you wish that you could achieve more? For some this could be a desire to just squeeze a little bit more out of life, - for others the urge to keep pushing ahead with plans and schemes, but in too many cases barriers, often self-made, emerge that thwart forward progress.

This is a book that will take you on a journey of discovery revealing how to reach your true potential so much more effectively. It is based primarily on a workshop I ran over many years for a wide range of participants, and which had constant success.

For many it was life -changing, - whether individually or business orientated. The text is full of personal experiences, - which give it a validity that transcends mere theory. It does and will unlock potential. It seems only right to share what I have found so helpful.

The concepts behind "Unlock Potential" had their genesis with my involvement with the British Junior Chamber (BJC). Taking part in an "Effective Speaking " seminar, and being impressed with the success of the local trainer, I then went on to become a finalist in the National Speaking Competition in Belfast in 1982.

With this experience I developed my own course, with a strong reference to Mark Anthony's famous speeches in Shakespeare's "Anthony and Cleopatra", and was able to successfully train others, especially with my key phrase of "Express don't impress".

What grabbed my attention was that everyone was amazed at the transformations that were taking place, - with each encouraging the others, - everyone was realising an ability they had not recognised was theirs.

Seeing what could take place from these sessions, I went on to develop my seminal workshop "Unlocking Potential". This led to presentations at the Junior Chamber International World Congresses at Birmingham (1989) and Kobe (1994), and to the European Council for International Schools in Denmark (1996). Loving what you do and what you are was certainly resonating with my audiences. The continued running of the effective speaking courses added further zest to these seminars, each benefiting from the other.

All the while I was maintaining an active and successful career as a Chartered Accountant, progressing to become partner in the Coventry office of an international firm. I became involved with training, and was the firm's official link with BJC.

The underlying motivation of love and respect for others led to appointments as President of the local BJC, and of the Warwickshire Society of Chartered Accountants. I was one of the original council members of Coventry Common Purpose and a co-founder of the Coventry Breakfast Rotary Club. My contribution to Rotary, and publication of the related (sometimes irreverent) prayer book "Amazing Graces", endorsed by the Bishop of Coventry, led to me being awarded the "Four Avenues of Service Citation for Individual Rotarians". Presentations of both the effective speaking course and "Unlocking Potential" flourished.

In both workshops feedback often included how refreshing it was to have common sense brought back into practical application, - ideas that could immediately be of use in the work place or at home, at university or school.

But were these just words? Seeing is believing. While my main occupation was as a chartered accountant I attended a chainsaw course, (I had a large area of woodland I wanted to look after safely), which was intended to provide successful participants with a certificate of health and safety in chainsaw use. Seven others were all experienced landscape gardeners needing this certificate for their work. It was for me physically very challenging. On the final day I suddenly felt a great love of the principles involved and for what I was doing. It wrapped round me. When we each took down our "exam" tree, - wider than the length of the chainsaws we were using, the examiner called everyone to look at the tree I had cut down, saying it was "the most perfect cut he had ever seen". I looked in awe of what had been done. The others on the course were simply amazed! I hope this one example (there are many others) shows what potential is present when love takes the helm.

Since my retirement in 2003 and move to Cornwall I have followed a different life style, a greater awareness of what love has achieved in my life and that of others. I have achieved most when I have thought least about myself, when love has been the pure motivation. Similarly, when difficult decisions had to be made, when based on principle and not self-will, this gave them impartiality, strength, and a recognition of fairness that deflected biased criticism. Unselfish love has been the springboard for continued achievement, involvement in local activities, and further success and unfoldment in the love of writing and sharing poetry.

So, why read this book? It is unique. It is a practical celebration of life and love. Each chapter can unlock the potential that is wonderfully yours, and can extend itself just as beautifully and inevitably to others - how much is your decision. It can be dipped into or read right through. Join the journey at any time. It has been travelled and proved.

And the first decision is to change in some way what you are presently doing, otherwise you simply stay as you are.

Take this key, open up your thinking and your life. Be aware that this book is much more, so much more, than mere positive thinking or visualisation. It is the reaching out and touching the potential that *is* uniquely yours, it is about proving the reality of your true being.

And a final thought. Unlocking potential is fun, - a joy to experience.

This book is written for you, - with love.

Ken G Cooper

Acknowledgements

I would very much like to thank three people in particular who have each in their own way have given invaluable support in the production and presentation of this book.

My valued friend Cate Vincent, who several months ago read a draft of the book I had first written some years ago, and urged me to take it up again, update it with my later experiences, and share it with world. Cate is a former management consultant, and her comments and encouragement have been most helpful. It was also Cate that recommended AuthorHouse to me, and the value of that recommendation is immediately evident. Thank you AuthorHouse.

Last year I was asked to be the Chair at the Christmas Concert of the Nankersey Choir, - one of the great Cornish male voice choirs, and a joy to hear singing. My main contact was Peter Thomas, - a very experienced company director, trainer and management consultant. We had a most enjoyable introductory chat, many of our thoughts and experiences were similar, and it seemed logical a few months later to ask him to review my book and make any comments. A very worthwhile dialogue ensued and has continued, and much helpful advice on presentation was generously given. Peter kindly agreed to write the opening words, for which I am indebted.

My dear wife Sue has been my constant support since we married. Her love is a gentle theme that runs though the book, - for it has given strength to my actions and encouragement to keep going when I forgot the goal and let problems get in the way. My successes would not have been possible without her, both in terms of looking after our two boys, and being the rock and foundation of my (and her) own desire to love and help more wherever possible. Sue has also read through the book and given most helpful observations, both from her good grounding in English, both at school and as a teacher, and also from her own recollections of the personal stories I have used to give validity to the focus of this book. Love indeed unlocks potential.

Thirsty?...What's Your Goal?

A CUP OF COFFEE AND BEYOND..........

A seven year old boy was attending a dog show with his parents. When the first interval arrived, his mum asked him to buy her a cup of coffee from the canteen hatch 40 yards away. The little boy was delighted with this responsibility. He had never been asked to do something quite so important. He took the 20p his mummy gave him (it's an old story!), and, chest filled with pride, went off to do as he was asked.

So far so good. He gave in his order, paid the money, collected the cup of coffee with its saucer, and began his journey back. Unfortunately, he hadn't gone very far when some of the coffee spilled into the saucer. He did what you and I might well have done. He slowed down and took greater care, staring hard at the coffee in the cup. However, he hadn't gone much further when more coffee spilt into the saucer. By the time he was just half way the amount of coffee in the saucer was excessive, and his enthusiasm was definitely waning. He was nearly at a standstill.

It was at this point that a kindly gentleman sitting nearby saw his predicament, and called to him "Hey lad, stop looking at the coffee, look where you are going!"

I was behind my son at the time, and I was delighted to hear him thank the gentleman for his advice, but then I was astonished to see the impact of his obedience to what the man had said. David looked at where his mother was, and fixing his gaze on her, while maneuvering round various tables and chairs, he went straight to her! He reached his mother in less than half the time previously taken, and I think without spilling any more coffee.

So what was it that David had done? Hadn't he achieved more with less effort? And isn't that something that we all wish to do? Indeed if we are to use the vast potential that we have, then achieving more with less effort is essential.

Let's assume, for the sake of argument, that we are using 50% of our potential. Let's also assume that we are working 12 hours out of every 24 in the day. It's fairly simple to argue that to unlock the rest of our potential, all we need to do is double the time we are working to 24 hours!

But no one can work for 24 hours a day for any period of time. Perhaps one might reach towards 100% of their potential merely by working harder, but if we cannot significantly change the level of the work we are doing, we need to change the *way* we work, individually and collectively, if we are to achieve our goal of unlocking the potential we have.

WE HAVE TO LEARN TO ACHIEVE MORE WITH LESS EFFORT.

The good news is that rather than *having* to do this, it is something each one of us surely *wants* to do, and can do.

Some years ago a student shared this common sense "I didn't realise the obvious fact that if I achieve more with less effort I have more time to do those other things I want to do."

So let's accept achieving more with less effort as a common goal. Let's remember what the man said to the little boy: "Don't look at the coffee, look where you are going!", and let's re-phrase his comment into a general and quite challenging statement:-

"Don't look at the problem, look at the goal".

When alligators are trying to bite, the problem is snapping right behind you! When cash flow is pressing, getting the money is urgent. At times like these, our focus may be entirely on the problem. We forget that the only reason we have a problem is because something has got in the way of our goal, our original direction. Problems certainly focus thought, but do they focus thought on problems, or solutions, or both?

Take the alligator example, for instance. Too close attention paid to the alligator might prevent us from seeing an escape route. We'd be looking behind and not in front, tripping over ourselves! To focus on the escape route will give us more chance of survival than thinking of the size of the alligator or of its teeth! Awareness of the challenge facing us is important to ensure it is dealt with. Often, however, we can become so mesmerized by the problem, so caught up in fear, that like the frightened rabbit caught in a car's headlights, we freeze rather than act!

How much time do we spend fearing and picturing what might happen rather than doing what is required ? How frequently do we find that once we have done what was required, the fear was misplaced, and was a total mis use of time? Had we had the confidence of there being a solution, how much more could have been achieved in the time spent worrying!

When your thirsty, isn't the goal to find something, anything, to quench the thirst? But how often do we specify that we need, for example, a glass of lemonade or lager, and miss the cool drink of water that is readily avaiable. We often make our own shortages, set our own conditions, confuse what is the true goal.

What happens to the problem when the solution has been found? The solution answers the problem. In fact, to the person with the solution there is no problem! Often when the solution comes, we might think how obvious it was -" I could kick myself"- is a fairly common expression. The solution had always been there, it just hadn't been perceived. How often we chide ourselves because if we had known the solution or had more confidence that the solution existed, we need not, and would not, have worried!

Let's take a look at the principles of mathematics. It took me a little while to master simultaneous equations, - indeed I recall getting upset when I couldn't master what others were achieving. However, the principle was unaffected by my ignorance. You could say **there is an underlying principle that governs everything we do. We might not understand it, but it is there.** Our views of it may change, but the underlying reality of that principle never changes. We aspire to it, not the other way round! The perfect equation is unaware of any problem. It is the solution exemplified.

The same is true of potential. It is always there. Unlocking potential is all about seeking the solutions which exist. The solution may not be what we had in mind! It's very practical, because if we find the answer to a situation, we have removed the problem - and it becomes a stepping stone to fulfillment rather than a barrier.

The goal in unlocking potential is nothing less than to reach a greater understanding of our very being, to discover the underlying principle of life that governs all in perfect harmony. When we love what we do, love our job, we already have our hand on the key of progress. It opens up otherwise hidden opportunities. If we seek the source of all intelligence, surely everything else has to follow.

Those that seek to understand their true source will unlock what that source provides. For many this is the very existence of an infinite God, who knows all. The phrase "Seek ye first the kingdom of God" follows this line of thought. It is logical on this basis to agree with the book of Proverbs, in which it states "those that seek me early shall find me" (Proverbs 8:17 those). Others may seek this source through meditation.

Whatever direction we are coming from, if we could only align our lives, our businesses, to this absolute and governing reality, we will experience a wonderful level of activity and purpose. We would begin to unlock more of what we truly are. When we reach out to others with an unselfed love, we find the beauty and power of the universe.

One of the most influential and well known people in history is Jesus. And for those who are conversant with his life, one might also think of this comment in relation to the unlocking of potential: "He that believeth on me, the works that I do shall he do also; and greater works than these shall he do; because I go unto my Father". (John 14:12). Greater works than these can be done by those who seek the source of all things, who seek the Father of all.... **When we identify our true source, we identify**

our true potential. Each of us will have our own perception of what that true source is.

The Bible is focused on that source being God. It says"God is love; and he that dwelleth in love dwelleth in God, and God in him". Whether you believe in God or not, there is no dispute that Love is very powerful, and that is the power that will unlock potential as nothing else can.

So let's establish our goal as unlocking that potential we have. Look forward confidently to the joy of achieving more in our lives and the lives of others, by proving this power of love.. When we let love take control, our potential is simply awesome. That is proved.

These chapters will take you along a well-proven route that will reveal to you more of what you can certainly achieve. Read through in sequence or dip in as you will. Every step has its varying views and opportunities. Wherever you start, it is taking the first step that is so important, and the second will follow.

Full potential is always waiting, beckoning you. All can drink from the source of life.

Love will guide you all the way.

THIRSTY?...WHAT'S YOUR GOAL?

SUMMARY

+ We can all achieve more with less effort.
+ To unlock potential requires change!
+ Solutions are not aware of problems.
+ Don't fixate on the problem, look for the goal.
+ Our goal is to unlock potential, to love more.

Turn the key.......drink in what is waiting for you: be led by love.

Climbing Mountains

SEEK AND EXPECT A SOLUTION

Imagine that you are at the foot of a mountain, and the order has been given to climb to the top. Let's imagine too that the spot where you are is at the base of a sheer rock face with an overhanging ledge that hides the rest of the mountain from view. There are very few hand holds, the wind is starting to whip up, and the rain is lashing down, causing you to be buffeted against the wet rock wall. *"Climb the mountain"*.

The problem is the sheer rock wall. The required result, the goal, is to be at the top of the mountain. For many of us life can be like that, we aren't where we want to be, - being caught at the base of a mountain with no route of escape, no sign of progress, and with an impregnable overhanging ledge that prevents us from even seeing where we want to go. We can feel trapped in our little section of the world.

Sometimes our problems seem insurmountable, and we can become transfixed. So we spend an enormous amount of energy struggling, slipping, moaning, and becoming more and more despondent as time ticks by with little or no progress made.

What is one to do when faced with these solid rock walls in life?

Whenever faced with any kind of problem, it is vital to *seek and expect a solution*. It has already been provided, and just needs to be seen. It may not be what you wanted!

FINDING WAYS ROUND THE PROBLEM

There are three broad ways "round the problem". *Firstly*, the individual, (or the team or organisation), can decide to go to the left, or to the right, or alternatively to stand back from the rock face, and see that there *are* different viewpoints and approaches that can be taken. Note well the classic phrase "I would not start from here"!

Secondly, if the individual is transfixed by the problem, *it is possible to ask for help.* This is not a sign of weakness, but a recognition of team strength, turning to what is available. This team can therefore be both at a human level, - organisational, including family, or at a spiritual level, when the individual turns to meditation or prayer. How many times have people struggled and struggled because of vanity, or false pride, or because of fear of being cast as failures, when a simple request for help would have dealt with the matter quickly. How many organisations have a culture of setting people up to see how they cope? How many people find a solution when they put aside the clamour of the problem and find, in stillness, an answer revealed. For those who turn to God it would seem logical that God has already got all the answers, if we are brave enough to listen. If you do not believe in God, perhaps there is an acceptance of an underlying undefined consciousness that often through the stillness of meditation, as with prayer, brings solutions to thought. The answers are there, irrespective of what one beleives.

So, getting any help *is simply reaching out to the help that is already available, to existing experience.* It really is not necessary to re-invent wheels in order to learn effectively. The amount of time, bother, and frustration which is consumed by the unwillingness to seek help, especially when that help is waiting to be given, (-"Why didn't you come to me sooner?" is often followed by "Is that all that is required?"), is time wasted, opportunity lost. **There is a balance to be struck between asking too quickly, and too late.** Whenever the balance is taken, help from another source is always available.

Thirdly, one can check out whether the goal is still relevant. In the present times of rapid change, what may have been important yesterday could well have been overtaken by new events or information that changes the goal posts. How quick are we to respond, individually or collectively? Are we on the right mountain?

THE IMPORTANCE OF ATTITUDE

Remember that in dealing with challenges, in climbing the mountains of life, our attitude will determine the altitude we reach and success obtained.

In fact, our attitude will determine whether we even want to climb the mountain, whether we want to progress in what we are doing, or not.

I was told this story years ago. It concerned a group of people who spend their lives wandering round the base of a mountain. One day they come across an individual who is standing at the foot of a pathway. He tells them that the pathway leads up the mountain, and each step gives better and better views, while the view from the top is truly magnificent. The people say that they have not seen him before, and seek confirmation of his job. He replies that his only purpose is to point out the path. They thank him kindly, and indicate that it is something they would like to think about, that they would carry on walking round the base of the mountain while they gave this their consideration, and would get back to him. When they finally return the man is gone, and they cannot see the path. The original opportunity is no longer there. A fresh one must be sought.

Who is it that stands at the base of your mountain pointing the way to go upwards? It is <u>not</u> your colleagues, best friends, family.

It is your own consciousness, your thought. For a path is always there.

All the time we seem to be struggling with a problem, the opportunity to find the solution is present. If we stare at the problem, that is all we will see. If we seek the solution, and open our thought to its revelation, we will see it when it appears, and will be able to take the path required. *It may not be apparent if we are not looking for it. It may not be the solution we wanted.*

One of the strange paradoxes that we face is that often we get accustomed to "our" problem, and despite the fact it is causing us a challenge, it is a known commodity, with which we have become comfortable. Other people may be sympathetic, and add the "reality" of that problem to our situation. It is seen as something to struggle with, and will take time to overcome. The recognition that there is a solution may in fact be unwelcome, because the problem had in fact become our goal, our focus, and once it is dealt with, we have lost our goal in life! Hence the clinging to the problem that has become our best friend!

Like potential, solutions are waiting to be dis-covered, whether we like it or not. A challenge that exists for some problem finders, rather than solution seekers, is that the solution may have become apparent, but it is not the solution that that individual wants.

The pure solution is one that gives what might be called the "right" answer. To be discovered we need to ask the right question! This needs us to be alert to every situation. So:

More good news! We exist at the standpoint of opportunity. We only have to turn round and there are 360 degrees of different perspectives *at that level*. The joy of walking up the mountain is that each step higher gives grander views, and gives more control of the situation.

The paradox is this: **Solutions are easier than problems, yet we sometimes still prefer the problems! The path to the side of the rock face is much easier to climb, but are we really ready and willing to climb it, knowing it leads to the unlocking of the potential that we have.** It may simply be the fear of change, "the devil you know", the fact that any change we make is a risk, -"I've not done that before". **Progress requires us to do things we have not done before.** This requires a progressive attitude, an open and fearless mind.

Progress is looking forward. and implies there is a goal to which we are heading.

STEP BY STEP PROGRESS

My family and I climbed Cat Bells in the Lake District many years ago in the Easter holidays. It was a difficult climb in wet, windy weather. Half way up the goal of the mountain top seemed impossible, yet we knew it was there! And it would be found! The immediate requirement was just to take the next step. And then the next step. Step by step. As we took each step, we were one step nearer our goal. **When the overall objective seems too large to deal with, tackling it step by step is logical, because that is normally how it will be achieved.**

Sometimes, rather than one step after the other, it is possible to jump, or leap. Sudden insight, lateral thought, spontaneous interaction in team situations, can propel one towards a solution far faster than a step by step process would envisage. In both literal and metaphorical terms, a helicopter flight will be faster than on foot. We may therefore get impatient *waiting* for the short cut to appear, *wanting* the short cut to appear, but perhaps not entirely convinced it will. Holding out for the possibility, rather than acting upon the certainty, is a subtle form of procrastination or complacency. Step by step both gives the expectancy of progress and a deeper knowledge of detail.

BENEFITS OF PATIENCE AND IMPATIENCE

There is a simple difference between patience and impatience. Patience comes from knowing that the objective will be met at some point, and that each step that is taken is moving one in the right direction, even if some of the steps slide backwards. Perfect patience is knowing "To every thing there is a season, and a time to every purpose under the heaven." There is fulfillment to the goal in which you believe. If you love something, you will demonstrate patience, because the goal is clear and desired.

In contrast, impatience is being involved in activities, time, effort, when you believe the outcome is not going to be achieved without immediate action, or indeed when there is no certainty of the goal. Perhaps just the desire to be doing something! It can be a lack of trust.

There are important lessons here for the importance of communication, and bringing a team together. **A patient team tends to be focused and confident. But patience must not become complacency. An impatient team may well need re-alignment, it runs the risk of wasted effort, but it can also be one that gives impetus when complacency sets in....**

As stated at the outset there is a balance to be struck. While patience may win the prize, it may require the initial impetus of impatience to get things moving. What kind of person / team most represents you?

REACHING THE PEAK

If my family had no goal in climbing the mountain there would have been no achievement nor any purpose. As it was, we were focused on the summit, and each step became a mini-victory, an identifiable element of progress. We became astonished at how far we were progressing. Amidst the deep and heavy breathing, the increasingly panoramic view gave new insight to the advantage of seeing things with the attitude of altitude. Our love of what we were viewing began to take over the physical effort, which became strangely less and less. That is what love does.

When we finally reached the peak, we cheered. We were rewarded with the completion of our goal as a team, the exhilaration of the view, that fleeting feeling of being at one with nature when all consciousness of effort had suddenly disappeared. We were at one with our goal.

All the other peaks around us stood as further challenges. Like potential, they stood beckoning irrespective of our wish to climb them.

The joy of unlocking potential is like the joy of learning, - the more you know, the more you use, the more you want to find out more, to do more. **There are always other peaks to climb**, rivers to cross, other horizons to stretch towards.

While unlocking potential requires the constant re-vision of the peaks there are to climb, we are free at any time, and should make ourselves the time, to stand still and enjoy where we are and what we are currently doing.

THE BENEFITS OF "PEAK" PERFORMANCE

The person at the top of the mountain has more control than the person at the bottom, for two key reasons. One, he has more vision. Two, he can see what is going on. Leadership and management require this global view. Let's ask ourselves the question, - aren't we all involved in both leadership and management in most aspects of our lives? We certainly need to manage ourselves, to watch what we do. Leadership may be more contentious, but in so far as everything we do is an example to anyone who may be watching, we have an influence, be it great or small, on the world around us. If we are performing at or close to our peak, doesn't that then become a "good" example to give? How happy are we to take on the responsibility of leadership?

Another illustration we can take from the mountain is to consider the effect of mist or fog at the base. If there is a fog layer, one can go for miles along the bottom of the mountain, and remain fog bound. Yet at any point one has the possibility of rising higher, (and it may only need to be one foot higher!) to lift out of the fog and see clearly the direction to go.

When driving through fog progress has to be slow because you cannot see where you are going. Unless you have a form of radar, you have to drive within the distance you can see. In these circumstances it might be well to examine the options.

Why spend all the energy, effort, and danger, in going at 5-10 miles per hour, and taking hours to complete a journey, if the fog will lift in a few hours time? Is the journey, the struggle, really necessary? What else could you be doing in the time? Wouldn't the journey be safer and more enjoyably taken if you can see where you are going? Sometimes we can achieve more by just being still and waiting for the quiet of inner inspiration to guide us on our way.

REACTIVE OR PROACTIVE?

Reactive styles are those which respond to problems, the trouble shooter fixing the urgent problem. Proactive styles are anticipatory, and plan for events which can be foreseen. Logically the person who is higher up sees more of what is going on. In a hierarchical sense the manager, for example, should know more than the shop floor worker about the wider issues; some decisions will not appear to make sense because often not all the facts have been given, or are known. While the person at the top has the broader view, let's not forget however that the person on the rock face is the best placed to describe the detail. Each situation has its unique balance to be struck to find the solution, but we can say with confidence that it is better to be more proactive than reactive.

Reactive styles tend to get caught in, or dropped in, the fog. Proactive people see the fog coming, and have already planned their way round it (or above it!), or in some other way sought an alternative plan. Our original questions are relevant, - what can I do from a different perspective, can somebody else help, do I need to tackle this problem in this way at this time?

All this requires communication, and the recognition that the views of everyone are important. This is unlocking potential with love, because to love your fellow worker / colleague / contact is to give them full respect and appreciation. That is a powerful influence. More on this later.

Solution seekers are proactive peak performers, they want to achieve more, and they find solutions. Problem finders find problems. Which of the two achieve more with less effort? Which of the two are more in control most of the time? Which of the two do you think you tend to be?

Haven't we all at some stage in our lives had the marvellous experience of looking at some achievement, and declaring with amazement, either to ourselves or our friends, "I didn't think that would be possible". Think back to what made it possible......

As we work through this book, we will be taking our own steps that lead inevitably nearer to finding our peak performance, revealing the fresh views of each mountain we climb, unlocking potential.

CLIMBING MOUNTAINS

SUMMARY

+ Seek the solution. Focusing on the problem is a misdirected and wrong goal.

+ Look where you want to go, imagine yourself at the mountain top.

+ The higher our altitude and attitude, the more control we have.

+ Progress begins with the first step. Leaping plays its part.

+ Be part of the solution, not the problem............ which am I?

Be a "peak" performer.

THE TRAMP AND
THE VIOLIN

COVENTRY MARKET

A friend of mine, John, was a market trader in Coventry and for a number of years he sold various *bric a brac*, and made a comfortable living. Now John is an amateur musician who plays the violin with more enthusiasm than skill. One day he bought an old violin in a job lot of items. As far as he could see, it was not anything special. He cleaned it up and tuned it, and put it on show, thinking he might get £20 for it.

However, during the course of the next month, no one even seemed to look at the old violin.

On the Friday, a tramp walked by his stall, and noticed the sad old instrument, looked at John, and asked his permission to play the violin.

If you had been John what would you have said?

Some people say "No", most others "Yes", and a few are undecided. There was a risk involved. No one apart from the tramp knew what was in his mind - he could have been wanting to run away with the violin, smash it up, or play it! John considered for a moment. It had been a boring day so far, with nothing special happening and he felt he hadn't much to lose, and might have more to gain. So he said "Yes", and passed the violin and bow to the tramp. As he did so, he felt a tingle of anticipation as if something strange was going to happen.

It did.

The tramp took the bow and violin, and gave a deft flick of the bow against the strings to satisfy himself that it was in tune. Then he set himself, took a deep breath, and began to play.

How to describe the next few moments! In simple notes that spoke to the very heart of all around, the music spread like a ripple across the whole of the market place, the tramp and the violin became as one. It was as though they were deeply in love with one another, each seeking to bring out their best and joyously share in each! The depth of expression, the sheer enchantment that was woven and woven in the folds of musical tapestry! For five glorious minutes the market place was still, enraptured in the excellence and pathos of his heart's overflow. There were tears in the eyes of many people, even in those of my street-wise friend.

At the end of five minutes the tramp could take no more. He suddenly put down the violin and vanished into the crowd. Someone called out "How much for the violin?" John responded "£50". A rapid auction took place. The violin was soon sold for £120. I would have bought it for twice that and had it on display for all it represented!

These events crystallized in thought some key facts regarding the nature of potential.

✦ THE ONLY THING THAT EVER CHANGES IS THE *UTILISATION* OF WHAT IS ALREADY THERE.

This is such an important point. So many people believe they have to change their potential if they are to succeed, but this gives a sense of incompleteness, and it is entirely wrong! The violin had the same potential whether it was played by the tramp, Yehoudi Menhuin, John, or any one of you. I like to imagine the violin thinking (!) as it sees a variety of people pass it, "Play me, play me, use the potential I know I have!" And depending on who is passing, and who picks up the violin, will depend the potential which is used.

Unlike the static violin, we actually have a say in accepting who we let into our lives, and how much of our potential we are willing to use. It is an intriguing risk, as it can be life- changing. When Jesus said to Peter and Andrew at the start of his ministry "Follow me.." it was indeed life-changing, - "and they straightway they left their nets and followed him" (see Matthew 4:19-20). That was some ask. It helped change history. Had that been you or I what would have persuaded us to do exactly that? Is there anyone for whom you would even now be prepared to leave everything if you had the belief it would unlock the potential that is there? For the religious person, how prepared are they to leave *everything* for God?

Just think for a moment, - who would be your "guru"? What would you expect to learn if you spent a day / week with that person?

That potential is within you even now.

That potential is unique to each one of us, and is beckoning

each one of us individually (and organizationally). Like the mountain top, it is only waiting to be discovered, and climbed.

May I suggest that the tramp reached out to the violin with love, - he saw in the violin its true nature, and knew what was possible. Here let me take a step into fantasy to make a point. Can you imagine the violin for a moment as another being, - like someone who has been cast on the scrap heap of life and has lost all feeling of self worth. I can imagine it thinking (here's the fantasy) "Play me someone, play me, I know I can give something !" And when the tramp gave of his love, the violin responded. What we are seeing is the parable come to life, because the violin is just like you or me, yearning in our lives to do better because we know we can. So when the opportunity arose, the violin gave of itself. I believe the same was true of Jesus and the disciples, and is true of any leader and follower. The potential is waiting and yearning to be used.

If you love climbing, you'll climb more mountains than someone who doesn't. The mountains are waiting for you. How much of the mountain is climbed, how much potential is used, how much love is poured out, is your decision.

We decide, have the right to decide, and have the responsibility to act upon:

- -- which mountain we target
- -- whether we climb the mountain, or not
- -- at what point(s) we stop and establish base(s)
- -- how far up we aim to go
- -- how many mountains we will climb

Events may need to happen to make our potential more

accessible, but the potential itself never changes. While anyone for example has the potential to be on top of Mount Everest, (-*any one*, given the money and resource required, however unlikely, *could* be lowered by helicopter), this is hardly a practical proposition. But the example demonstrates the possibility. We *have* that potential. Whether we want to be there or not is irrelevant regarding the *potential* to be there.

What makes *our* potential unique to us, however, is that what we can each achieve is unique and special to each one of us. We each have our own mountain, our potential, that looks down and says climb me because I am there. And as we climb we see more and more of the vast potential we have. We may not be able to run 100 metres in ten seconds, or be the managing director of BP or president of the TUC, or a porter in a hospital, whatever, but we all have the potential to find that niche in life which gives fulfillment to what we uniquely are. It is there.

We all have our mountains to climb. Let's take the encouragement that the first step begins our journey, and the second brings us nearer.

Whilst every individual has unlimited potential, so too does every team and organisation. It has the uniqueness and individuality attached to its people. Hence the common sense of "Investing In People", drawing out the vast potential which exists and needs only to be used. Every organisation has the *potential* to be world class. Every organisation should be asking the same questions we saw above.

We come back to the introductory story, and the importance of *looking* where we are going. To be effective, this requires us to *know* where we are going. And the answer can be for all of us **"I'm going to reach out to fulfill the potential I know I have.**

With all the potential that is uniquely mine, I know that with the right help I can achieve it!

As mentioned previously, do you have someone with whom you would like to spend time, just knowing that they would lift you up to out-perform what had previously been expected of you? Someone perhaps from the past who has already spurred you on to achieve more than you thought was possible, and may be able to do so again?

This takes us back to the story of the tramp and the violin, for we ask a second question. "Who unlocked whose potential?"

The obvious response is that the tramp unlocked the potential of the violin. True. But didn't the violin provide the opportunity to unlock the potential of the tramp, and to exactly the same extent?

✦ WE UNLOCK OUR POTENTIAL AS WE UNLOCK THE POTENTIAL OF OTHERS.✦

This should be the crux of the entire desire to unlock potential. The moment we begin to feel that we cannot do any more, or that we are unlocking a sufficiently large enough percentage of our potential to rest on our achievements, might we not look at the world as a whole and ask the searching question, how many more people in the world could I help?

A very successful chairman of a company once said to me that he was using 95% of his potential, and that I should not tell him otherwise! The company had done extremely well and he was working 18 hours a day, enjoying every moment. He could not work any harder. But more could have been achieved and with less effort by the simple act of delegating. Giving others responsibility builds their performance, and in so doing the overall performance of an organisation has to improve. He did not and would not recognise that others on the Board felt great frustration that he did not listen to their ideas, - he trusted himself rather than trusted them. His hard work was very well rewarded for a short time, but eventually became too much for him to handle. His company crashed.

Good delegation unlocks potential by significant margins, and vice versa.

Good delegation requires a good knowledge of the people involved. Such time spent with staff pays ample dividends, especially when one finds out what others love to do, for then it will be done well! It releases one's own time, and enables others to achieve more, and to want to achieve even more. This also includes within one's family! To let them reveal more of their potential is to love them, - one could say as a parent loves their child.

We unlock our own potential as we unlock that of others. . As we see our potential, we should love to see the potential in others used as can be encouraged. From an organizational point of view, this crucially involves unlocking the potential of staff, customers and clients. Good delegation requires good knowledge of those involved. It requires the giving (and accepting) of responsibility.

Full commitment to our customers because we care, will not only have the benefit of customers "for life", (full commitment must mean exactly that!), but will contain within it the growth of both the customer and one's own organisation

Again, this is not confined just to people, but to every object that exists and even to every invention still to be discovered. The computer has enormous potential but until it is switched on the potential is dormant. Once power is given, it can perform. (Have we switched on ourselves, our customers!?)

Now, the software I have bought for my computer contains far more than I will ever use. However, an expert could use my computer and get far more from it than I do.. The potential is there. It needs only to be used, - and in a way each one of us is like the computer software. The potential is enormous, but are we brave enough to use it? Are we willing to be trained to get more from what is available?

I was self-taught on the use of the EXCEL spreadsheet, and was reasonably proficient. When I worked for an international charity, that proved helpful for the first four years, but I had struggled that year to clear an EU budget application on time. I was asked if I would like to do the Advanced EXCEL training course. Using advanced techniques, creating a budget template which included self-checking cells, so I could send work back that had not been properly done, I was able to complete five major applications in the same one month time span as the previous year. I had had no idea that that that was possible! Everyone benefited. It re-emphasized the value of training, - which is, after all, there to bring out the potential that we have.

And here just a plea, - ensure that all training is followed up, and the handbooks are not just put on the shelf and forgotten!! Too often training is provided to "tick a box", rather to actually help individuals. Effective training requires effective communication, - a close knowledge of the individual needs, a desire to see that the training is indeed followed through and made effective. This follow through should be done within weeks, and with full feedback.

Just to emphasize the point, one day of tailored training, followed by a week of planning and putting into practice, increased my productivity 500%. And was, of course, great fun! I achieved a lot more with less effort.

And another point arises. Had I had that training four years previously, or once I had settled into my new job, that increase in productivity would have happened that much sooner, and rippled though all I did in the subsequent years. I had not known that various techniques were possible, that I could do them, and would enjoy using them. When I shared the new templates with the finance staff across the world, everybody benefited . We helped each other.

It is the responsibility of management to ensure that staff are suitably trained, and for staff to ask the open question at any time, not just during staff appraisals, is there any way I can do what I am doing more effectively?

This is the joy of the learning process, seeking how to do better by working together. What makes giving seminars special is that they are all different because the participants are different and the expectation is always that everyone learns something new. If the presenter did not have that expectancy, the seminars really would be dead affairs.

Let's go back to the example of the tramp and violin.

In our lives we are both tramp and violin. We are both able to unlock and be unlocked, often by far more than we realised.

Who else had their potential unlocked in that incident?

The crowd of people who watched and listened I feel sure would have had their day enriched. They had been touched by excellence, and that touch would have been reflected in their performance for as long as it was in their thoughts.

John, the market trader, received £120 when his expectation had been £20. So, he had undervalued his assets just as we tend to undervalue ourselves, and not only had he witnessed the event, but he was both materially and mentally richer in consequence.

Yes, we unlock our potential as we unlock that of others, - and so we have the tramp, the violin, John, a large number of people, all unlocking their potential, because John said one little word that took just a second to say.

"Yes."

How often do we say "No", when we could say "Yes"- and why? Because, regrettably, "no" is the instinctive response to most situations. Don't take a risk. Don't do that. Think of the negative consequences. Think of the problems.

And once "No" has been said, it tends to be definitive, thus closing down genuine opportunities..

Of course, sometimes "No" *is* the right answer. Sometimes saying "no" can unlock more potential, freeing us to perform existing commitments more effectively, or prevent a detrimental situation developing.

How much better, though, as a general rule, to think instinctively "Yes". How much better to open the door to opportunity, and then discuss the opportunities. Why not let "Yes" be our instinctive thought, reflecting that there are answers to all problems, to think "yes" first, and look for positive solutions. "No" can always follow, if appropriate, and may be given with an alternative solution, but if "yes" is your instinctive attitude with which to challenge situations, you will have a more positive and helpful response overall.

Let's go back once more to the tramp and violin. Before John could say "Yes" the tramp had to ask him a question.

And what did the tramp need to do even before he asked John whether he could play the violin? He had to find the right person of whom he should ask the question, and he had to know what he wanted to do, pluck up courage, all these things, but fundamentally he had to perceive right at the very beginning, the possibility of playing the violin. Without that there would have been no music, nothing would have happened.

So then we have:

✦ WE HAVE TO PERCEIVE WHAT WE WANT TO ACHIEVE. ✦

This goes straight to the heart of unlocking our potential., because although our potential is already before us, if we cannot see it, we will not be able to unlock it. **Vision precedes action**. Necessity is the mother of invention and all inventions are merely (!) the dis/covering of what is possible, they are the realisation at a particular moment in time of what has always been possible. Necessity drives us to seek solutions to problems. It provides the impetus that forces new ways of doing things. The burning desire to succeed is effective simply because the antennae of perception are fully raised, probing for any solution that is or can be made at hand. Solutions exist even when undiscovered, and we have the sure knowledge that once perceived, achievement can certainly follow.

I was chatting with our builder about dealing with challenges, and he said to me "If you can imagine something it's possible". We gave him the task of building a barn, - something he had never done before, -he'd never had to do anything like it! What he came back with, and built, was unique and very practical. He imagined, and made it possible. We all benefitted. Perception is the essence of invention, discovery, the excitement of challenge, the daring to believe... What do we imagine? What fills our thought first thing in the morning? How do we perceive ourselves and what we will achieve today?

If we were to improve our perception of ourselves we would improve what we accomplish. This is a fact.

To put this another way, **we do not need to change what we are, we only need to change our perception of what we are.** As our perception moves into line with the reality of our true potential, we will be able to express more of that potential in our lives.

Let's be clear about what we are considering. We are not seeking to visualise what we would like to be, (notwithstanding that for many people visualisation is very effective), but to actualise in our thinking what we truly are. Put another way, to follow out train of thought, it is possible for a violin to visualise itself as a trombone, - but what's the point of that? Far better to see itself for what it is and glory in that uniqueness. Perception isn't about invention, it's about understanding what is true. (See the next chapter!)

Now isn't a painting the perception of the artist made tangible to others? Whenever we make anything, don't we want it to reflect our best thoughts? Isn't it a reflection of how we see ourselves, and how we want others to see us?

The opening book of the Bible refers to God's declaration that "He saw everything that He had made, and behold it was very good." Don't we all have that yearning for fulfillment, whether religious or not? Another angle may well be to ask how a mother views her baby / child? Surely with great love, and with the expectation of providing anything that will help that child progress. Would a loving mother leave her child to gather dust, like the violin was left? No, - because her perceptions would be, to use the simile of the tramp and the violin again, to see her child play....

So let's ask these telling questions:

How do we perceive ourselves?

How do we perceive one another?

How prepared are we to love ourselves and others to really want to unlock the potential that we and others undoubtedly have, - not as a duty but as a deep desire?

THE TRAMP AND THE VIOLIN

SUMMARY

- Unlocking potential generally means saying "Yes" rather than "No". Sometimes "No" is the right answer.
- Our potential, and that of others, is like love: it is unlimited.
- The only thing that ever changes is the *utilization* of what is already there.
- We unlock our potential as we unlock the potential of others.
- We have to perceive what we want to achieve.

Let's make music together. Let Love be the key.

THE IMPORTANCE OF
PERCEPTION: WHAT
IS REALITY!

HISTORICAL LESSONS

Our perceptions are of vital importance.

Some 2000 years ago Julius Caesar was getting ready to invade and conquer Britain. His battle hardened soldiers were prepared to venture forth, but for all of them there was just a little bit of apprehension. Everyone knew that the world was flat. The only problem was where did it actually end. A kindly soothsayer came up with the answer. Her comments, translated from the Latin (!) were "Beware! Britain is at the extreme edge of the world!"

Had we been in Caesar's army at the time, we would have believed this to be true. Any proposed exploration of the limits would have been extremely cautious and each onward step perceived as fraught with danger. Yet, all the time, it was their fear that was groundless, and not the world.

Just over 500 years ago, (1492), Columbus set sail West to

reach Asia. For 1,500 years the false perceptions of a flat world had largely remained, and were still to the fore. Imagine with me Columbus going to see his bank manger with his adviser nervously at his side. "What do you want, Columbus?" "A loan for £100,000" "What for?" "I'm going to sail West and reach Asia". It would have been a brave bank manager who would have risked the bank's money and the ridicule of his colleagues.

Yet someone did believe him. Someone eventually backed him. It was the reluctant Queen Isabella of Spain, who had been told that this would enable her to become the greatest queen in Christendom. Someone, it was Isabella,, said "Yes".

His perception was that it was possible to sail round the world and reach Asia from the West. The only way he had of proving his perception was to prove it.

The only way we can ever prove anything is to <u>do</u> whatever is required to prove it.

[This was very clearly brought home to me years back when I had given a seminar to core staff of a major advertising company in London. The chairman was concerned at my using the word "love" at all, - but after the workshop had finished, his gratitude was expressed in giving me some advice he had always found very useful, - dare I say, loved: "the only way to do something is to do it!". Deliciously simple, - I often think about it when prevaricating, - I both love it and hate it!!]

So, back to Columbus, who first had to perceive the possibility of actually sailing round the world. .

It did not matter that nearly everybody else did not believe him or the possibility. The simple fact was, as we now know, the world always was round. This is and was the truth. Wasn't it therefore inevitable that someone, it happened to be Columbus, would prove its reality. The world did not become round as Columbus sailed round it. **The reality was always there to be proved.**

It took a long time for perceptions to change. Yet they had to because the reality of the situation had to become known. The freeing up of perceptions and the willingness to consider new horizons was surely an important factor in the Renaissance, and they are equally important now.

Similarly the Book of Revelation in the Bible is exactly what it says it is, - the revealing of what John believed and saw to be true. His new heaven and earth became his new perception of reality, and if true must at some point become the reality for everyone . How far can we see in our lives, department, organisation a new self, department, and organisation transcending present limitations? Asking this question made the workshops both fun and fulfilling!

What lessons can we learn from history?

Our perceptions form our reality, and we always act in accordance with what we perceive and believe.

History is written on the same basis.

PERCEPTIONS, - LIMITING OR LIMITLESS?

What present perceptions do we currently have that are limiting what we do, but in "reality" are actually wrong? In one hundred years will people be looking back at amazement at what we currently believe to be true?

In physical terms I can perhaps reach no further than my outstretched arm. If I need to reach further, what am I to do? Thought can reach out to infinity. If I bind myself to my physical abilities, I bind my possibilities. If I stretch out with consciousness, I reach beyond the stars. Moreover, my potential is more than I can perceive at this time. If we are still, and listen, can we also see a new heaven and earth that beckons, the reality of our true potential?

We begin to unlock that true potential only as we reach out to what is possible, and by challenging the so-called impossible. Once perceived, it is a step nearer to becoming a reality. We can then focus on the new possible. It is a step by step process, one foot at a time, one mountain at a time. I am reminded of Apollo 13, - an impossible rescue achieved because the impossibility of not seeking a solution was never accepted.

PERCEIVING REALITY!

As long as we keep searching and seeking out our potential it is inevitable our "reality" will be proved, because it *is* there to *be* proved and demonstrated.

As Columbus showed that the world was round, so too shan't we prove at some time that we are what we truly are, unlimited, boundless in what we can achieve!

The classic Age Of Discovery in which Columbus lived is wrong to limit itself to a particular period of time, because every second of the day new discoveries are always being made, whether on the global scale, or in the minutiae of living, as we learn new things about ourselves and our surroundings, as we each come to understand more about what is real.

What makes potential so alive with magic and promise is what might be called **THE LAW OF DISCOVERY: WHATEVER EXISTS, CAN BE FOUND!**

The Bible states it more succinctly: "Seek, and ye shall find."

The unique potential which each of us has, exists. It can therefore be found. If we seek out that reality, it is inevitable that our FALSE perceptions and limitations will fall away as we move into line with the TRUE PERCEPTION of what we are, in other words, what we really are. Complete. Fully rounded.

A friend hearing The Law of Discovery commented "Whatever does not exist cannot be found!" If we do not believe we have potential, it does not exist in our thinking, and while we think in that way we will not find it, until perhaps a tramp, or a Jesus, or a St Paul, walks our way.....it was always there.

Whatever reality may be, it is there, irrespective of our beliefs, and that reality is there for each of us to prove. We may each have different perceptions of it, but **"true" reality is independent of changing perception, dogma, argument.**.

Let us remind ourselves of two of the themes from the tramp and violin. Firstly, the only thing that changes is the utilisation of *what is already there*. Secondly, we do not need to change *what we really are* (true reality), we only need to change our perception of *what we think we are* (perceived reality) to what we really are. The violin had probably never had such beautiful music played on it before, and we have that same possibility.

To use what may sound somewhat grandiose, in the orchestra of life we are each needed to be what we truly are for the grand composition to be properly fulfilled! This is perhaps what John of Patmos saw in the book of Revelation.

More of reality is discovered when potential is unlocked and fully expressed True progress is dependent upon our moving into line with reality, - it makes sense, as it can be found, to *seek* the reality of our potential, because we are then moving in accord and harmony with what might be called our real being, and expressing our real freedom.

Something of this was glimpsed when the tramp and the violin became as one and something is glimpsed whenever any of us become so engrossed or inspired in what we are doing, that we lose all sense of physicality, and transcend to higher levels of performance. It is the difference between the mechanical and inspirational. Some people call it operating "in the zone."

Last year I was coxing a gig boat with six crew. We were rowing on the Carrick Roads, - a beautiful stretch of water in the Falmouth estuary. We established a perfect rhythm, "reaching and laying", "reaching and laying", the oars were all clicking against the pins in absolute unison, and we were gliding effortlessly through the water. We all felt at one, and it is a memory that will last forever.

Potential when unlocked beckons this higher level of existence and performance. Unlock the potential of anything, and we approach performance at its ideal level.

It is not possible to unlock the potential we have unless we change the way we do things. This will usually require a change in what we perceive as our true selves, and surely our

ultimate goal is expressing our true potential, in other words, finding, discovering, the reality of what we can achieve.

GETTING BACK TO REALITY! BEING PRO-ACTIVE

There is a very practical expression which may be going through your thoughts at this point. "Let's get back to reality" or more starkly "what planet are you on!!" and this is a more important statement than we may realise! Which is more practical, preferable, and effective?

1. re-active management / problem solving.
2. pro-active management / solution seeking.
3. "perfect management", (yes, I did use that word!) -full potential sought and expressed. This is surely the objective of continuous improvement. Perfect quality management(PQM) is one step beyond total quality management(TQM) – seeking out what is perfect. Rather than react, let's just ask how can this be a helpful model? For that is exactly what is has been.

Time after time in the seminar sessions the question "what would be perfect for you / team/ organisation" led to ideas that opened up new avenues of thought and possibilities that were seen as being within reach, ideas that delegates had not previously wanted to share, or lacked faith that they would ever be considered.

It is generally accepted that proactive management is far better than re-active management, and as we become more proactive we find that our horizons increase and expand. Continuous improvement is the buzz word of the day, and it is our stepping stone to the recognition that our potential is continually beckoning us. The law of discovery is the driving force behind continuous improvement and what makes it possible. To seek continuous improvement is very powerful and exhilarating.

During the course of any one day we will find situations which allow or demand pro-active or re-active responses. The target must be to steadily increase the number of situations where we take control, to start each day with the expectation of finding new opportunities because they exist to be found.

The further you look ahead the faster you can go. In driving a car, the focus ahead has to be a function of how fast you are travelling. A car travelling at 1 m.p.h. can in fact be quite dangerous because the driver will not be able to see immediately in front of the wheels at that slow speed. The inertia is considerable, any increase in speed requiring considerable effort. One is almost required to drive with the foot on the brake ready to stop in an emergency. There is little vision. It is a re-active situation. As the speed increases, the vision expands, far more is achieved. The risk of blow out or need to swerve remains, and may call for a re-active response, but within the confines of the example, a more pro-active position is achieved.

Similarly, when playing a musical instrument, it is not possible to sight read effectively by looking at just one note in front of where one is playing. That is reacting to the immediate position, and would be slow and jarring, with no feel for the composition. One needs to look several notes ahead, to encompass in a general vision the notes and instructions which have been scripted.

How pro-active do I wish to be? How far ahead can I perceive and still retain control?

The way to discover what we can do is to let our present

perceptions move up a gear, and drive, play, accordingly. As we continuously progress we will develop a pro-activeness in all we do.

Potential is only unlocked as our perceptions stretch us forward to do what is possible, to discover and express the reality of what can be achieved! Eddy wrote in her seminal book Science and Health "Perfection underlies reality", and more provocatively "Without perfection nothing is wholly real". Startling words at first, but a fitting conclusion to this section, - the recognition again that our potential must be seen as our reality, that the underlying reality is surely good..

Seeking perfection is very powerful, - it is what love naturally seeks .

Perceptions: What is Reality!

Summary

- We live in accordance with our perception of reality.
- Perceptions change. Reality does not.
- Our perception of potential unfolds as we progress towards the demonstration of what we truly are.
- We cannot unlock our potential if we cling to limited thinking.
- Pro-active management allows the individual/organisation to take control, and move more securely towards their goal.

Reality is there to be discovered, and is more readily found by those that seek it.

DEFINITIONS AND PARADIGMS

THE IMPORTANCE OF CLARITY

Perceptions of the same thing differ. The challenge of any form of communication is that what one person says and means may not be what the other person hears or interprets. Hence the importance of continually checking that we are talking the same language, i.e. understand what the other person means. The only ways to do this are to ask questions or restate in one's own words what others are trying to say..

It is very challenging, and may sometimes be thought demeaning, having asked someone to do something, to ask that person to say in their own words what they have been asked to do. It is a risk. Your pride that the other person didn't really understand a word you said!!, or their pride that they pretended to understand but really didn't. We have all experienced both sides of the coin. Think of all the wasted effort that has been caused because of false pride, simple mis-understandings.

There have been many times when I have sought clarification at a meeting, and participants have later thanked me in private because they did not understand either. I am indebted to my wife, for sometimes I would get carried away with jargon, and she would ask "What do you mean by that" or on one occasion simply "Why?" And that made me re-think a strategy for which I had made a number of faulty assumptions.

Rather than fear criticism the atmosphere whether at home work or play needs to be one of support, and how to provide encouragement or not will unfold in this chapter, starting with what we mean by "potential".

DEFINING POTENTIAL

Ideas from seminars have included such phrases as

> latent / lurking possibilities
> caged energy
> the capacity for improvement / development
> whatever is possible
> the inherent potential to come into being
> present / future power
> the route of continuous improvement
> what can be perceived.

While improvement is possible, there is still potential to be realised. If we were seeking to *fully* unlock all the potential we have, (and surely we should be that adventurous!), this would continue to drive us to seek out those situations where finally no further improvement was possible. Wouldn't that be perfect!

Put another way, **isn't the fulfillment of the potential of any situation what might be called the perfect solution at that particular moment?** The paradox of experience is that when we have achieved what might be perceived as "perfection" in one direction, or with one objective, other demands, goals, challenges appear. As we have seen, having climbed one mountain, others come into view. When they have been climbed, the stars then wink and tease... Yet it is only by seeking perfection, however we may define it, that we can hope to begin to fulfil the potential we have.

The word "perfect" does cause many of us to recoil, yet it can be used effectively as a friend, and not an enemy. Doesn't it make sense to **seek what is perfect for you in <u>all</u> the circumstances?** This throws out the problem of perfectionism, which loses sight of the main goal in the minutiae of individual less important goals. It also recognizes the value of stretching perceptions to identify the ideal. We need to emphasize the importance of getting the balance right.

Reaching and achieving an objective, scoring 100%, is a perfect score. I have just watched again the performance of "Bolero" by Torville and Dean at the 1984 Olympics, remembering that it was scored as perfect by all the judges. They fulfilled the potential of that occasion and that dance. Watching any sport / activity done at that level is a thrill, and it was a thrill to watch it again, knowing I was watching something considered perfect. Reaching into the ultimate performance is possible in other areas: it may be a long term target, but jewelled with the expectation and reward of constant progress.

A working, and purposefully challenging, definition of potential could then be "the *capacity* to express perfection", and one could add "in all the circumstances", stressing the importance as referred to earlier, of seeking the perfect balance. My memory of coxing the gig boat, described earlier, was perfect for those involved, but an expert may well have found fault. It would not have mattered to us.

From a Biblical point of view, to be thought provoking, the simple command to "Be ye therefore perfect....." demands from those that wish to respond to this command the total fulfillment of the potential God gave them. In the Biblical sense, perfection can only be found on a spiritual level. For the Buddist, finding perfection is the ultimate destiny. For the scientist or physicist, the unlocking of potential contains within it the deep questions of understanding reality.

Any unused capacity to express perfection remains as latent, lurking, and still possible.

Irrespective of one's point of view, isn't it an inspiring and challenging and logical goal to seek to express perfection because if we can ever find perfection that is our true destiny. The main reason for *not* wanting what is perfect is not wanting to be spending time at a perfectionist level? But if we seek the perfect balance that will not arise. Why accept unused capacity when something more perfect can be envisaged / perceived under all circumstances? Why not go for it? As we use more of the potential capacity we have, we shall recognise that there is more to discover. Why unlock potential? Because it leads us closer to the "perfect" performance, which is waiting to be found.

How can we move towards this in a practical manner?

A "PERFECT" MANAGEMENT TOOL.

As Earl Nightingale indicates, if we accept that what we can perceive and believe, we can ultimately achieve, it is axiomatic that the way we think determines our success, *and the speed of that success.* The vision of what is possible becomes the attracting force that both drives and motivates, and **the model we have**

in thought determines what we will experience and what we will impact upon others. The appendix gives a listing of what I have designated "PERFECT" and "IMPERFECT" words, used as acronyms. This has been used with great success to identify what is being thought at the time. Clearly there are many other words that could be included, and very many that would not start with the letters we have! Nevertheless, it provides a logical model that has worked very well in seminars, and reference to a selection of the words shown will demonstrate some of the potential that is within them.

Let's summarize some of the "**PERFECT**" words now, and look at a few in particular:

Professional	Positive	Persistent	Practical
Effective	Efficient	Enthusiastic	Energetic
Responsible	Respectful	Reliable	Responsive
Fearless	Flexible	Friendly	**Forgiving**
Excellent	Encouraging	Enterprising	Ethical
Communicative	Caring	Committed	Confident
Trusting	**Team working**	Truthful	Tolerant

BEING PROFESSIONAL

Who would not wish to be perfectly **professional** in their work? We each have our different perceptions as to what that might mean. The conscious thought, "How can I do what I am currently doing more professionally?", or "How would the perfect professional plan my day ahead?" are simply means of stretching our thoughts to perform better. **In thinking more professionally, we act more professionally.** A valuable question we can ask is "How can I be more professional with the use of my time?" Seek out being 5% more professional in what you do for the rest of this day and you open up its achievement. It takes just a few moments of quiet thought.

Soon after my appointment as a partner, the managing partner came into my office, and caught me thinking! I had my hands clasped in front of me, and was deep in thought on ways to improve our marketing strategy. I will always remember his words."What are you doing! Get on with your work!" Good activity isn't necessarily expressed in physical terms. As noted later, being professional also requires trust. I was setting a professional goal, but he couldn't see what I was thinking. However, set no goal, and the lack of improvement is also achieved.

BEING EFFECTIVE

The second letter gives us **effective.** The word originally used in the unlocking potential seminars was efficient, but *one can be efficient doing the wrong thing.* A management committee at a school requested the P.R. officer to produce an advertising video within one week. The officer, one of the teachers, worked extremely hard and with great enthusiasm and produced what she thought was a first rate 15 minute video just in time for the meeting that was planned to authorise full production. As the video was played it became apparent that it was not at all what the committee had in mind, and they decided not to go ahead. The individual had been very efficient in everything she had done. The result was in fact what could be called negative effectiveness, - no goal achieved, feelings of guilt and frustration. Achieving more with less effort requires clarity of goal for all those involved, an agreed perception of what will be effective.

A recent seminar came up with the following definition of how to be effective. *"Don't rush into a job. Relax, and take a little time to think what's the best way of doing it. Then do it."* This was said by the youngest member of the group, and wasn't it brave and lovely!

BEING RESPONSIBLE

One of the most important requirements in the unlocking of potential is the acceptance of **responsibility**, whether it be from an individual / team / organisational position. The classic phrase *"If it is to be it is up to me"*, is telling. We'll come back to this a bit later on, but for now it's worth noting that it is the "responsibility" to our true potential that helps us take the initiative when things need to be done. Leaving the first move to someone else may just be a way of finding someone to blame if you don't think the goal will be achieved.

Taking responsibility for an action is a mature approach which finds its confidence in the rightness of the ultimate objective. Its added strength is in knowing that right action is independent of personality, and can be pursued with the sure knowledge that any attack or criticism is really an attack on what is principled, and not on the person, and the principle can take care of itself! I have found this a great support when standing up for what is right, and deflecting personal attack as not in truth an attack on me. Other people, if they are being professional and effective, will give their support.

When no one takes responsibility, and there are plenty of examples of this, it is very hard to go forward, damaging both individual and organisation. Too often one can pedantically tick the boxes of what is expected, but no-one then takes responsibility for what is "outside " the box. I would far rather tell someone they are responsible for an area of control than give them a detailed list. It has been proved how much more successful that is.

BEING FEARLESS

One of the most powerful factors in locking or unlocking potential is the presence or absence of fear in an individual or organisation. Individuals who are fearless are usually those who believe in their vision. Fear of failure is a desperate trap. A principle of a college said to someone who was being asked to do a difficult assignment, "Go and do it even if you get it wrong!". The look of relief on the person's face was clearly visible. The fear had been taken away. She did a first class job. Recently a top snooker player was commenting on the failure of many very skilled players to make the top grade, and he put it down to thinking of the consequence of leaving a pot open if they missed, rather than straightforward confidence in making their shot. The nagging fear not dealt with by playing percentages with confidence meant their potential was never fulfilled.

There is a balance to be struck between fearlessness and caution. Blind fearlessness is dangerous. Alertness is wisdom. If fear takes control, we lose our freedom to act. If we are to progress, risks will have to be taken.

Any learning *is* a risk; it is doing something not done before, and if we determine never to make a mistake, we will be determining to do nothing worthwhile in our lives, because we will never dare to unlock the potential that is waiting before us. Everyone is aware of the phrase **"Practice makes Perfect"** and while we are practicing we may make mistakes. But with each mistake shouldn't there be the expectation that we are getting better and better. The way to correct a mistake is to keep practicing until the mistake no longer occurs! Then we will do it right when it matters. However, a word of caution. Practice also makes permanent whatever you repeatedly do.....

There is another fundamental that must be shared, and that is both Biblical and obvious to any who have experienced its meaning."*Perfect love casteth out fear.*" Why? Because thought is turned 100% to the object of our love, and fear has no place to reside. When love overcomes all your thinking and action, fear is rarely to be found as a limiting factor. More on this later.

BEING FORGIVING

How much time is wasted when we fail to forgive, not just others, but more importantly ourselves. The apathy and the wallowing that comprise self condemnation are major enticements, but **every second spent in self condemnation is a waste of time, a mis-use of resources, yet how often do we all so indulge?** Better surely is the commitment to learn from mistakes, to see them as stepping stones, and then make those stepping stones to progress.

We must accept that what's done is done (serenity), learn from the mistake (courage to admit and change), understand what needs to be done (wisdom), and then get on with it. We must put the past behind. We cannot climb the mountain looking backwards! **Where we are going is more important that where we have been.** If we can forgive ourselves, we can also forgive others. Many will recognise the following from the Lord's prayer: "*forgive us our debts, as we forgive our debtors*". Forgiveness is, quite simply, freeing and beautiful.

However, mistakes need to be identified and rectified. **If we**

have learned from our mistakes, we have earned forgiveness. If we have not learned we will repeat the error, and we and or others, will suffer in consequence. There is no unlocking of potential for someone who will not learn from mistakes, and this then becomes a challenge of attitude.

The prayers just mentioned are powerful. There is tranquillity in forgiveness., and the central religious figures in history are our models. We can have the serenity, the courage, to forgive right at this very moment…….. One of the most far reaching of all religious sayings is *"as ye would that men should do to you, do ye also to them likewise."*. This is one of the most powerful business tools I know., - simple, effective, and easily understood. That's not to say it is always easy to do! One can forgive and love someone who has cheated you, but there is no need to do repeat business!

BEING EXCELLENT

A favourite word is that of **excellence.** It signifies the striving and achievement for the ultimate, the peak of performance, the thrill of experiencing and being involved in something excellent. We come round full circle to the value of setting perfect goals. What is perfect for you or I has within it the pursuit of excellence, perfect performance. There is a joy which everyone shares in watching anything which is done at the level of excellence. This joy transcends envy in the thrill of recognizing magic moments and it gives an indication, a perception, of the excitement that stems from unlocking potential.

BEING COMMUNICATIVE

Continuing our look at PERFECT words, how good is our **communication?** Is it effective, merely efficient, or perhaps even deficient! The lack of effective communication is one of the most frequent reasons for failing to use the potential we have. In simple terms, *we often fail to communicate with ourselves by not giving ourselves time to think things through,* and so we fail to dis-cover the potential that is there.

Good communication takes time to ensure it works, bad communication takes less time initially but leads to wasted time subsequently. We all know the phrase "Think before you speak" and it is a good one!

More obvious, perhaps, is the crucial point that communication should be for a reason, and all too often the lack of a clear goal makes effective communication impossible. Too often meetings are held out of habit, have people in attendance who need not be there, and fail to clearly identify the action that needs to be taken and by when.

There is a persuasive view that thinking positive means not sharing what is called bad news. **But this kind of positive thinking per se is dangerous. Ignoring problems never helped anyone. And we solve them, we deal with them, by focusing, clarifying and agreeing our goals.**

Remember that lack of communication when there are difficult challenges leads to rumours, falsehoods, fears. Such negative attitudes can be so easily avoided. If management can put problems into their true perspective, (i.e. that there is a solution!), it becomes a matter of **trust** to recognise that everyone has a common goal, - the success of their organisation, and will fight for it if they know what they are fighting for! Hence the great value of mission statements when they are more than just words!

If everyone is seeking solutions, there is simply more opportunity to find them. Communication, chat, discussion needs the focus of the common goal, not gossip and rumour! If we don't lead communication from our strength of knowledge, the "devil" will lead it from fear and doubt. **Who is communicating to you? Who are you believing?**

BEING TRUSTING

We need to earn our trust of one another, and this can only develop through supportive and open communication. It requires the development of shared values.

How much trust is there within your organisation / department. This really is a key issue, in which the trend of tracking / regulating / monitoring can make one feel management is always "snooping". Discussing this with an employee doing some repair work in our home, it was clear this was a burden that hung over the morale and the freedom of honest performance. Seen as a sledgehammer to crack a nut, if there was honest team work there would be no individual taking selfish advantage. If there were, the other team members, in loyalty to themselves and their standards, would in the past be able to deal with the situation. Red tape was not always necessary!

Good team work requires good communication and trust, and this involves everyone. It also requires honesty from everyone. A good business friend told me that his success in dealing with awkward situations was based on the realisation by staff that he would always do his best for them. The turnaround in improved staff turnover when I became a partner in a national firm was on a similar basis. Because I was willing to spend time with them, I got to know them and vice versa. There was mutual trust. This brought significant change. Let's just note that the communication and trust has to be genuine!!

This was brought in to relief recently when chatting with a local trader. He mentioned the phrase "practice what you preach". He was fed up with those people who read their text books, tick the boxes, and falsely believe when they say the right things that that is effective. I have taken many interviews where the interviewee has clearly been on an interviewing course: they know the words, but it is evident the words do not come from the heart. Who wouldn't rather take on someone they could trust than someone who was good at learning mere words! "Techniquing" now includes conveying the "right" attitude: and the question has to be asked "How much do I trust this person?" Reversing that, I wouldn't want to work for an organisation where what was said was deemed more important than what was felt and meant. As the trader said, far too many people do NOT practice what they preach, - and the effect on morale, effort, all the good things one seeks, is obvious. It may be interesting just to pause at this point, and think of examples where words are said but not meant.

Just a little and powerful example may be added here. We can combine both trust and effective communication across all nationalities and borders without a word being spoken or written. The smile, yes, the *genuine* smile, when conveyed through the eyes of fellow feeling and true affection. When you have given a smile to someone, the number of smiles in the world do not decrease by one! I've never known anyone to run out of smiles. You can smile whenever you want! Like potential, smiles are just waiting to be discovered and used!. Like potential, smiles are free. An honest smile is a demonstration of trust. A dishonest smile has no place in a good heart.

BEING A TEAM MEMBER

Another T word is worth sharing: **TEAM**, and the simple acronym **Together Everyone Achieves More**. The recognition that each of us has a different perspective to offer, that each of us, no matter what job, position, responsibility, qualification, has the potential to offer insight to any situation. As we have seen earlier, the potential to share ideas, to have a sense of humour, to enjoy each other's company, is always there to further the potential that lies within.

When you are part of a team, you fight for them. You give your all, and that is reciprocated. Is there such a team spirit within your family, place of work? Do you feel that spirit of love that, to take the thrust of Biblical and religious tenets, reaches out into world brotherhood? Indeed this is beyond religion, - it is the essence of love that in any situation can come to the fore to help one's neighbour. It is the highest response when we fulfill what we truly are. It is the truism we all know, when we work as a team the result far exceeds the sum of the parts. It is exhilarating, powerful. It simply shows what can be done when we help one another from the heart. We have all proved it.

What we have just done is to take seven or eight words based on the word PERFECT and focused our thoughts on the implications of letting those words be part of our thinking. If we look at the words in the Appendix we will see that there are a variety that can be considered. Given a different scenario, one could discuss what the key words are for you own organisation or self, - they may be quite different from the ones described above. However, they all have some very important features in common. The dynamic and fascination of running seminars is that each group attracts to it the words it most needs and indeed symbolises, and the more openly they are discussed the more powerful the resulting teambuilding, support and action that results.

All the words shown are words which entail giving. They involve other people. They are unselfish, outward, solution based, and, like the smile, they can be given and never run out. In simple terms, they all have the power and inevitability of unlocking potential.

How far do we wish to see them evident in our lives and experience?

We return to the word "responsibility". It is a fact that as each individual in a team or unit expresses these words, the team in which they work will express them. As each team in an organisation expresses them, so too will the organisation.

The examples we set demonstrate our standards and expectations, whether individually or as an organisation. We are uniquely responsible for those standards.

We have therefore a two way process, which is the basis of team work after all. The need to set the PERFECT model in thought is both logical and effective. At any point in time the *balance* of the words represented will be adjusting to recognise the needs of that moment, and for any individual the makeup of these words will be different, reflecting their uniqueness and special contribution.

The word "balance" is crucial, because it signifies the perfect solution <u>for any given point in time.</u> What is right now will not be right when the underlying assumptions or facts change. Plans should always be flexible for this reason.

When we fill our thoughts and therefore our actions with the perfect words we have been looking at, and there are of course many others, we move ourselves and our family / business through to seeking what is perfect in our lives.

Tall order? It really depends upon what we wish to achieve. It can be done. I have witnessed it.

NOW BEWARE!!

IMPERFECT Management

Is there negative potential? Words and their related actions that lock up the potential that we have abound! The appendix shows a number of them and some of the key ones are now listed

Potential Killers!

Insincerity	Intolerance	Insolence
Mediocrity	Minimalism	Mendacity
Procrastination	Personality	Pettiness
Ego	Escapism	Evasion
Ridicule	Rumour	Revenge
Falsity	Fear	Fashion
Exaggeration	Envy	Easefulness
Cowardice	Can't	Cheating
Thanklessness	Techniquing	Temptation

Casting our eyes over these words we can see how easy it is

to let them become part of our thinking. Worse still is the recognition that we can see people, departments, sometimes whole organisations that seem to express these qualities.

Working with one group of people, with the flip chart recording their perception of IMPERFECT words, an accurate picture was built up of what was actually going on. The shock of recognition was sufficient to break the spell, the mesmerism, that was affecting performance. What happened? It was agreed that the sheer common sense of the matter was to stop doing all of them! And the way to help that happen was to replace the IMPERFECT model with the PERFECT model in our thoughts. That began a ripple effect that spread throughout the organisation over the course of a number of months. It transformed the organisation, (the workshop was the last throw of the dice by management!) and what was looking like inevitable failure was turned to success.

At any point in time we have the option of which way our thinking is going, we decide what goal we want before us.

Each one of us has the right and potential to say "I used to be like that. But no longer". Let that be of the past. Fact. Cannot be changed. What can be changed is the NOW. Live the NOW to the full. The three prayers mentioned earlier are powerful in putting the past behind us, **on condition that previous mistakes are corrected,** - and indeed part of the serenity comes from knowing that we can change our attitudes **right now.**

All these words are like seeds growing in a garden, which we could call ourselves, our organisation. The perfect words are like ground cover plants in the sense that enough of them will keep out the weeds, but if we let the weeds grow, they can choke the good plants before they are established. How important then to root out any weed before it grows. How easy it is, for example, to let resentment grow in our consciousness, until it becomes an all consuming dragon! Or to let procrastination prevent everything being properly achieved and finished off! Seeds need to be nurtured, and for many the parable of the sower in the Bible will be well known, - good seed falling on good ground gives a good increase!, - in this case an hundred fold increase, - that's not bad!

The Appendix includes a poem I have written about "The Gardener". It is a simple celebration of the impact on ourselves of keeping our gardens tidy. And the reverse is surely just as true.

Problems, unwanted thoughts, dealt with when they are only tiny roots in our consciousness, are far more easily overcome at an early stage than when they are deeply embedded and entwined. Thought left alone, or treated as unimportant, can become almost part of the family, part of the furniture. The acceptance of a problem can sometimes be so strong that there is a resistance to deal with it even though it may be about to destroy you! It can become part of one's life, and we become comfortable with it, despite the fact that it is a potential killer.. The thought which takes root becomes part of one's way of thinking, be it a false habit, or a bad friend, and **we are known by the friends we keep......**

The person who is mentally alert actually sees a wrong thought coming before it takes shape and root in consciousness. Eddy wrote *"You must control evil thoughts in the first instance, or they will control you in the second."* This is vital because **all these IMPERFECT words are negative.** They are inward, selfish, they smack of either excuse, blame, and failure, or self importance, self love, the "I'm all right, in charge and you will do as you're told and as it suits me". **They are attitudes which implode on themselves, a kind of black hole attracting negativity and eventual destruction.** Surely then we should never allow such thoughts to fester in our thinking, or go unchallenged in the thinking of others!! They are a waste of time and energy. They truly are potential killers...We need weed them out while they are still small, - don't give them a chance to get into our consciousness.

Our challenge is two fold:

1) **to keep in thought those things we wish to experience,**
2) **remove from thought, weed out, those things we do NOT wish to experience.**

Again, this is not just a question of thinking in a positive way, - it is drawing our consciousness into the reality of our true potential, which the perfect words will release.

A CAUTION

We must never underestimate the importance of keeping our thoughts in line with where we want to go, **while retaining the balance of awareness and wisdom.**

A successful businessman, who had recently retired, shared with me his golden rule for any one who was to survive in business. "BE STREET-WISE". Although it is right to see in people their true potential, because it is inherently theirs, if that person is not yet known to you, or is in the habit of expressing qualities which are an offence to you, do not let them know the inner secrets of *your* mind until *their* inner motives are *fully* appreciated. **The serpent will smile, the scorpion will sting.**

One of the key PERFECT words we have already referred to is that of "responsibility". We are responsible both for the thoughts and for the people we let in to our lives. **It is not responsible (or professional, or effective!) to open wide one's door to someone who has *their own* best interests at heart to the detriment of yours.** Trust needs to be earned, and that takes communication and alertness. **The wrong kind of so-called positive thinking (mere will power) ignores the problems that need to be overcome.** The risk in believing what you *want* to believe is that you can effectively invite the robber into your mental home and it will be ransacked because that is what robbers do. PERFECT thinking includes responsibility. This correct thinking tackles the issues square on, and fights on the side of what is "right" until victory is secured.

We should not seek to run before we can walk.

This does not deny the need to have vision. It is a call for being prepared. The mountaineer will wear appropriate clothing, will be in training for what is expected to be tackled. If offered equipment at a cheap price, what value is placed on one's life if the offer is accepted without the wisdom to ensure the equipment is of the right quality? Why unlock the serpent's potential at the expense of one's own? **Sometimes one must say "NO!".** We must not feed potential killers, must not invite them to stay, must keep them far from experience. If we cannot deal with them at this point in time, we must take other appropriate action.

Why risk the challenge of dealing with adverse situations, threats, thoughts when we can get rid of them before they take hold? Destroy them by denying them existence in your experience, root them out at the earliest opportunity before they start to grow and insinuate themselves in your life!

This is the importance of one step at a time, controlling each thought as it comes to consciousness, moving towards the vision that we have, and with each step rejoicing in the proof and progress it represents. As our skill and confidence improves we are better able to tackle more challenging issues, and can do so with the expectation of success.

The serpent would love to nestle undisturbed in the undergrowth. Positive thinking might say "It will not harm me". That may work. But beware. We unlock the potential of others by creating the environment in which they can operate freely. The true thinker therefore is not just a positive thinker, but exposes the dangers which exist. **The solution is not to ignore the problem, but to remove it.** Seeing the negative influences as negative influences we must remove them from our experience in the most effective way we can.

If this means standing up for what we believe in, - the PERFECT words within each one of us, are our protection, strength and demonstration.

DEFINITIONS AND PARADIGMS

SUMMARY

+ Potential is the capacity to express perfection.
+ What we do expresses our standards and expectations.
+ PERFECT words involve giving and are positive. They are based on Love.
+ IMPERFECT words involve taking and are negative. They are based on self.

Perfection is the underlying reality of true potential. We get there together.

CAUTION

Life is about getting the balance right at any moment in time. Be street-wise, be flexible. Conditions change. Don't entertain what you do not want to experience.

FUNDAMENTAL LAWS

Fundamental laws are those which exist irrespective of custom, perception, parliament, whether we like them or not. Fundamental laws are friends or enemies depending on whether we work with them or against them.

They are like traffic lights on a busy intersection that are based on a time clock. They will go through their sequence irrespective of the volume, shape, type of traffic, that uses the crossing. While one moves in accordance with and in obedience to the sequence, there is harmony, freedom, flow. Move out of line with the established order, and chaos will ensue. It might be tempting to blame the lights because they were there, but the chaos would be self-generated, or caused by others. The chaos would not be the fault of the traffic lights.

This is itself a fundamental point. Obedience to the basic laws of life gives freedom. It is disobedience that takes freedom away. It is an act of responsibility to do what is right. Irresponsibility to do what is wrong. The fundamental laws of life are those which unlock our potential, and propel us to fulfill the unique role that each has to play.

Problems are not part of fundamental laws. The law itself is never conscious of its violation. It is only our false perceptions and wrongful actions that violate the law that is itself independent of our actions. These laws give freedom from all problems as we move into line with them. As we perceive the underlying perfection of our true potential, **our lives move into the harmony that the universal law represents.** The law of mathematics is never affected by a mistake, but the mistake, unrectified, will have adverse consequences.

The law of 2 + 2 = 4 is never affected by the mistake that 2 + 2= 5, no matter how many times that mistake may be made. Our true potential is never affected by mistakes about its existence or validity.

We unlock our potential as we move in accord with the fundamental laws of life which support it. Let's take a look!

The first has already been referred to earlier.

The Law of Discovery: *Whatever exists can be found.*

This can be adjusted to read whatever exists will be found, because of the law that follows:

The Law of Progress: *Progress is inevitable.*

Our perceptions have to move into line with what is real.

Reality is what is and must ultimately be found. As we express more of the PERFECT words we move in that degree towards the perfection that ultimately exists..

The Law of Self-worth: *You are what you truly are.*

There are a number of well known statements relating to this law:

"As he thinketh in his heart, so is he:"
"You become what you think about" (Many variations and sources)
"behold, the kingdom of God is within you."

We need to go back to our PERFECT and IMPERFECT words. If it was not made sufficiently clear before, let us make it absolutely clear now. You become what you think about. If the balance of our thinking, if the balance of thought in our office, management meeting, community, home, is imperfect, that is what we will experience in our lives, and that is the value we will be giving to our lives. The opposite situation is also true.

Are we therefore simply looking at the situation where we visualize the PERFECT words, see clearly what we want to see, and through strength of will power bring them into perception and fruition? *"You are what you think you are"*. Few people would dispute this statement, or the effectiveness of its impact.

But, dear reader, this visualization may well be effective, and has been so proved and recommended by so many, but it misses the all-important point: it is making one subservient to what you or another would like or wish to be / have. It is positive thinking, but there is something better.

Some years ago, a class of twelve year-olds in California were asked "If you could have a wish to be anybody in the whole wide world, who would you wish to be?" Everyone in the class chose someone famous, - apart from one little girl. When asked who it was she wanted to be, her response was simple **"I want to be me!"** Isn't that something we should all feel?

And doesn't this response get to the heart of why we want to unlock our potential? Because we know it's there!! And uniquely ours.

Why choose to be somebody else when all we need to do is be ourselves, by unlocking the potential that is uniquely ours.

Every single thing that was ever created has its own unique potential that can never be taken from it. Whether you, your department, your organisation. The fundamental fact is that **"You are what you truly are".** Irrespective of what you may think, perceive, how you act, behave, see other people, what you truly are can never be taken from you. It is summarised by the *eureka* of Self Worth:

"I AM WHAT MY POTENTIAL IS................."

It comes back to the simple question, - who made me? What is my source of being? For some the Bible can be a motivation. Let's think about origins. *"Beloved, now are we the sons of God,"* and then *"Can the fig tree, my brethren, bear olive berries? either a vine, figs? so can no fountain both yield salt water and fresh."* Jesus also said *"behold, the kingdom of God is within you.".* For many this is perhaps a recognition that within each of us is a diamond that we have not yet recognised.

Jesus is also recorded as saying something which unifies all Christians, and for some all peoples. The Lord's Prayer begins: "Our Father", - a fundamental acknowledgement of what they see as their true source, - and if we all have the same source, we all have the same intrinsic self worth.

"I AM WHAT MY SOURCE IS" conditions how we will see our potential.

Whatever the source is deemed to be, it will not be a "respecter of persons". A spring does not distinguish separate drops of water, give one drop preference over another. Every drop is important. If you took away all the drops, there would be no spring. You are as important in proving the existence of the source as every other drop.

When we seek to operate at the level of perfection, it's like an orchestra playing absolutely perfectly. To achieve this, every musician has to play their part, so the individual playing just one note on a triangle for example is as important to the overall performance as the pianist playing throughout. They each have the same responsibility to perform at their peak, and each deserve the same praise for fulfilling their unique role. It would certainly cause chaos if in the playing of a musical composition the violins began to play the part of the trombones or drums!

When we see and believe what we are, we should be in awe, and love what we see, **for we each have a unique and special role, and should glory in its fulfillment.**

The Law of Attraction: *Like attracts like.*

Like Attracts Like (many have written about this too)

Therefore all things whatsoever ye would that men should do to you, do ye even so to them: for this is the law and the prophets.

"Owe no man any thing, but to love one another: for he that loveth another hath fulfilled the law".

The law of self worth finds its inevitability in the law of

attraction. The thoughts we entertain in our consciousness or inner most thinking will find their expression in our lives. Are we going to have our PERFECT words as our model, or the IMPERFECT? Alertness to the wonder of our potential brings that wonder into our experience. That is the marvel, in its turn, of the law of attraction.

It can also be summarised:"**You attract what you project**".

Let's ask the following challenging question: when you walk into a room what happens? Does your appearance on the scene lift the general mood or reduce it? Does it lock or unlock potential? What would you like to happen? Some people by their very presence inhibit others by their indifferent or arrogant attitude, while others positively radiate interest and enthusiasm. How much do people look forward, or not, to your presence? What happens when they think about you?

My Latin teacher at school left me uninspired and bored. I did not do well, nor did the whole class! Only three pupils passed (I was one of them). Another class, with a different teacher, were all successful and with good grades. My English teacher was so enthusiastic about Shakespeare and Chaucer, it instilled a love for their writings that has never left me. If an employee showed enthusiasm I would always go with them the extra mile. It is instinctive. Remember, we attract what we project.

There are some very practical issues which should be faced at this point. If we continue with the above example, when you walk into the room you take with you a sense of self worth that you would like to see expressed by everyone else in their own way. It is part of wanting to see your organisation express *its* self worth and its potential, and for that reason all the staff within that organisation have a duty and responsibility to be part of that expression.

If an individual fails to be uplifted by the enthusiasm and professionalism of others, the law of attraction will still operate. The person who maintains a negativity, and who embodies negativity, will be an unwanted source of negative attraction, and it is *that* which needs removal from the work environment for *that* reason. **When you get rid of a negative way of behaving, which you must at some point, if an individual is so attached to it that they cannot let it go, that person must go with it, and they can be free to unlock their potential somewhere else in a manner that suits their mode of thought better.**

High standards attract good behaviour, and vice versa. It is the responsibility of management to ensure that the law of attraction sets the goal of high expectation. And the same applies within the family setting.

The Law of Expectancy: *seek and ye shall find*

"verily I say unto you, That whosoever shall say unto this mountain, Be thou removed, and be thou cast into the sea; and shall not doubt in his heart, but shall believe that those things which he saith shall come to pass; he shall have whatsoever he saith.

Therefore I say unto you, What things soever ye desire, when ye pray, believe that ye receive them, and ye shall have them."

The Biblical promise could not be clearer. It may well be the source of modern "visualization", but the key phrase is *"when ye pray"*, - when you align yourself to your true source, when you believe the laws of self worth and attraction, only then can the expectations you have be truly unlimited.

"You become what you think about". The "becoming" is an expectation. It is an inevitable fact. It is the cast iron guarantee to each of us that what we think will have its impact directly in our experience. What a challenge, what a comfort, that if we therefore align our thinking with what is true, if we model our thoughts on what we see as PERFECT, we will begin to see that perfection evidenced, and increasingly so as it fills our thoughts.

And this is undoubtedly true: **"What you expect to happen, does."**

Does that seem fatalistic? Far from it! It is the clear recognition that the thoughts which we entertain deep in our thinking are those that we really think about. The expression "I always knew that would happen" is self fulfilling. It's simply no good having all the surface words about seeing the potential, for example, in a student, when at the end of term the student fails, and you comment to other members of staff "I always knew that would happen". The labels we attach to others and to ourselves stick, and self fulfill.

We can visualize solutions, or we can really go that tremendous one stage further and actually *see* the potential in others, (as one might for someone they love!), and in that seeing believe it yourself. We each know what we truly believe. Our expectations will be fulfilled.

If we fail to set our own goals (expectations), they will be set for us by the thoughts of others.

IT IS IMPERATIVE THEREFORE THAT WE SET GOALS WHICH TAKE US IN THE DIRECTION WE WISH TO GO AND WHICH WE BELIEVE ARE ACHIEVABLE.

The simple sentence of that twelve year old girl said it all: "I want to be me". Nobody else. No other person's label, or puppet. Me, fulfilling the unique potential I have, in the way that will demonstrate the unique contribution I have to offer in the world in which I live.

There is one more Bible verse that just fits in so well. It complements the Law of Discovery (whatever exists can be found) by making that law self-fulfilling: *"Ask, and it shall be given you; seek, and ye shall find; knock, and it shall be opened unto you."*

Our potential is here to be found. It's source is Love, its fulfillment is love. When our hearts are filled with love, the world is ours.

WHAT YOU SEEK, WHAT YOU GIVE ATTENTION TO, IS WHAT FILLS YOUR THOUGHT, AND IS WHAT WILL FILL YOUR EXPERIENCE.

So, finally and inevitably:

The Law of Fulfillment: *What fills your thought fills your life.*

Now, a further caution! "Seek and ye shall find" is just so accurate! It is one to both love and hate! We all know it is true. If you want to find fault with someone, it is surprising how quickly when you have found one fault, half a dozen suddenly appear! All those IMPERFECT words suddenly come crowding in, killing potential faster than you can blink! The horror becomes that even when there is no fault to find, the malignant desire to find something will create its own demon!

Now the law of self worth has us looking at our source. The law of expectancy should do the same, because the creator looks after his own. An artist ensures his painting is kept in the right environment, the engineer his product is kept properly maintained. When we look at our true potential, let us also feel the assurance that our needs are also always met. Jesus said *"your Father knoweth what things ye have need of, before ye ask him."* Love protects, cares for, as a mother cares for her child. That is the child's expectation and comfort. When we love one another, we can be assured that we have a high expectancy of good, both being shared and revealed in ways we never dreamed.

What a source of joy it is when we supply the needs of another before they have asked, - when management or staff do something that indicates they are aware of the needs to be met, and quietly and joyously do whatever is required. The law of expectancy is also the law of fulfillment.

How important to watch the way we think, to set the simple goal of expressing the potential we have, seeking the PERFECT model in our lives, seeking professionalism, effectiveness, responsibility, forgiveness, excellence, communication, trust, whatever key words fill the needs of the moment. And the Laws of Attraction and Expectancy will bring them into your lives.

Fundamental laws are those which do not change. They are the essence of life, of being. When we associate ourselves to the source of our being, we begin to fulfill the potential of what that being is.

"In Him we live and move and have our being" If you believe in there being fundamental laws, you must also believe that your very being is also part of them.

FUNDAMENTAL LAWS

SUMMARY

✦	THE LAW OF DISCOVERY	Whatever exists can be found - POTENTIAL!
✦	THE LAW OF PROGRESS	Progress is inevitable. We control its speed.
✦	THE LAW OF SELF WORTH	You are what you truly are.
✦	THE LAW OF ATTRACTION	Like attracts like.
✦	THE LAW OF EXPECTANCY	Seek and ye shall find.
✦	THE LAW OF FULFILLMENT	The result of all other laws.

Fundamental laws exist whether we like them or not. They never change. We are part of them.

WHERE ARE YOU LIVING
- EIGHT CORE QUALITIES

Our thoughts are, in simple terms, where we live. No matter where our actual home may be, and whether it is under cardboard or in a mansion, to take extremes, the way we think will be the mental home in which we are living. The person under cardboard may be happier than the person in a stately home. The difference between our actual house and our mental home is that we always take our thinking with us. It is vitally important therefore to ensure that we live in the mental home that we choose. Our true home and the demonstration of its potential, will follow.

In this chapter, we are going to build a home / house constructed of values, and from the stability thus founded anyone can launch forth with great confidence and assured success.

We're going to build on the images we are setting. If someone comes to your house, and rings the bell, knocks on the door, whatever, when you go to open that door you have the choice of whether to let that person talk to you through the door, just open the door, or let them in.

To be specific, how prepared are we at any point in time to let other people into our living room? Are there things hidden away that we do not want others to see? **The really challenging question is how comfortable would you be in letting somebody else into your consciousness, your thinking!** Many people spring clean their houses on an annual basis. Do we ever spring clean our thoughts, - check what is in them, and if there is any dust, grime, garbage, "imperfect words", do we let them stay, think about cleaning them out as a New Year Resolution, or clean up what ever we do not want right now?

The best way of avoiding a major cleaning programme is never to get so dirty that the only way of dealing with the grime is never to need such a programme. As my wife will confirm, the time taken to clean muddy footprints is out off all proportion to the time taken to take off the boots in the first place. **Unlocking potential is achieving more with less effort, and part of that is the sheer common sense not to do those things which are likely to make work for no reason.**

How often do we try short cuts, not for the good reason of trying a better way, but for no other motive than laziness! The law of attraction rewards the lazy motive with ineffectiveness! Laziness results in additional wasted time and the further collection of some of our IMPERFECT words! How often do we struggle with the wrong tool because it is handy, finally get the best tool for the job, and do the task in seconds! We will all have our own examples.

What then is the remedy on offer? It is to so fill our thinking with the qualities that we wish to see expressed that

1) there is simply no room for unwanted thoughts to get in.

2) by the law of attraction, only thoughts which we wish to entertain will be attracted to our doorstep. Unwelcome thoughts will be rejected before they can take root.

When we open the door, we take on board the responsibility for what is let in. Let's go through a process of welcoming eight chosen core qualities. Others could be used. Let's also be aware that when we are looking at this model of consciousness it has a far wider implication than just for ourselves. In much the same way that we have been looking at the self worth of individuals, departments, teams, organisations and indeed our homes, each one has its own "consciousness", and it is as important that our organisation, for example, keeps out unwanted thoughts and attitudes as much as we ourselves.

1) Ethics

Our model now is that when we enter the front door of our thoughts, the first room we come to has "ethics" written on the door, - much like one of those name plaques that one can buy nowadays. This is one of the words that came from a workshop some time back. It is in the listing of PERFECT words to which we have been referring. To me, without the foundation and substance of good ethics, anything else we do becomes empty and meaningless. So what is "Ethics"? One definition is "the science of the ideal man", in other words what would the ideal man do in the circumstances? He would quite simply reflect ideal values, whatever they may be. Those ideal values would reflect our PERFECT words. The ideal man is the epitome of unlocked potential.

For most people, when they join an organisation, they have an expectation as to the broad values that will be followed.

Similarly, for most people, when they establish friendships, they have an expectation of the moral outlook and values that their new friends will have. In simple terms they will seek to match their own. Like attracting like. There will be an expectation that those values will be consistent and not change.

Over the course of many workshops a number of words have been put forward when examining the PERFECT model that relate directly to one's expectations in this area. They have been underlined in the Appendix, and for convenience some of the key ones are shown below. In actual fact, all the perfect words we have looked at are part of an ethical outlook, and would define a person of good and strong ethical behaviour:

Principled	Responsible	Respectful
Forgiving	Fairness	Freedom
Caring	Compassionate	
Trusting	Team-based	Truthful
Tolerance		

Kidder (see "How Good People Make Tough Choices"), included those underlined and added Love and Unity as what should constitute a global code of ethics. All the above words comprise core expectations which transcend international boundaries, in other words where-ever one may go, there is a desire and wish to see the above qualities evident in the day-to-day transactions of our lives. Sound ethics provides the foundation for any sound operation. It should be the cornerstone of our house. It demonstrates true love for ourselves and others. Take away these sound moral values, and you take away everyone's potential. Live them, and we all benefit.

2) Effort

Our opening narrative in this book was for the necessity to achieve more with less effort. Effort was nevertheless required There is an assumption in any team situation that every member of that team will be giving 100% effort. The Oxford or Cambridge crew in the boat race, and all supporters, would be horrified (I don't think that is too strong a word) if one of the crew only put in say 90% effort. Indeed 110% is expected and given. At this level there is no room for any lesser effort, and if we want to be outstandingly successful that is what we need to give.

For any given job, 100% effort is the expectation, and guarantees full attention to what needs to be done. **Isn't each one of us worth 100% effort?** Knowing that giving that effort will unlock the potential of both ourselves and our organisation, doesn't it make sense to give it?

But there is also another thought regarding effort, and it is part of the consequence of the fundamental laws. I have experienced that when my goal is clear before me, when I love to do something, the achievement sometimes appears effortless. I am sure we have all experienced at some time that our love for doing something has transcended effort and even overcome physical limitations. The answer to this paradox may be that we have to put all our effort in to being loving! We can refer to 110% effort, because when we put our heart and soul into our performance, we transcend the physical.

Yet sometimes too much effort is actually restrictive. When Queen Elizabeth was to celebrate her Golden Jubilee I determined to write a suitable poem. As the day of the Anniversary drew nearer, my efforts just did not get off the ground. I was trying to force something and knew the inspiration was not there. Sure, I was writing words and phrases that rhymed, but they were empty. Eventually I realised that my thoughts were too much towards me and my performance and not to the object of my poems. I decided to spend time in research on the internet of all I could find about the Queen's life. After several hours, I suddenly felt an overwhelming love for all that she had been through, witnessed, stood for, her loyalty and love. I found myself just writing out a poem that just flowed. With further thought, and the inclusion of suitable photographs, this was then sent to Her Majesty. Her Lady-in-waiting wrote back that the Queen was touched by the sentiments expressed. The effort was rewarded when it was forgotten. Herein is a quality of love.

3) Vision

The essence of this book is the lifting of perception not just to what may be possible through visualisation, but to the deeper and underlying perfection that is one step beyond. It is moving the focus to freeing thought to see what unlocked potential represents. Vision is the first stage, the perception of what is possible. Talking with a very successful architect just a few months ago, he shared that he would give his clients a range of options / visions of what his instructions suggested. This was his special talent, and he wanted to share with them the potential that was there. Much of his joy was that the final choice was often something they had not considered, - his vision was unlocking what was always possible, given the vision to see it. The directors has visualized what they wanted, but the potential was always greater.

How important, vital, is the need for true vision! I believe it

comes from stillness, tapping in to the intelligence that is our true source of being. It goes straight to the heart of knowing where we are going, and being open to the thoughts that then flow. It is the scene setter, the global decision, the direction we want to go. It is important because, depending where we set the vision level, it is often only at that level there will be initial agreement.

Again linking back to earlier comments it equates to the person standing at the top of the mountain. That person is more likely to be in control, both because they can see what is going on, and also because the visionary can set the overall direction. **Vision sets purpose and motive.** It is an essential requirement of leadership, for the more clearly the vision is seen and expressed the more confident *and effective* is the leadership. It enables the goals to be set in harmony with the underlying reality of our true potential.

It can be argued that visions are one step beyond goals. The latter are more focused strands of the overall picture. When I was appointed partner with an international firm of Chartered Accountants, my specific brief was to improve the standing of the office to which I was to be appointed. My vision was for it to be both the best office in the city in which our partnership then operated and in the national partnership as a whole. At that time it was one of the worst and staff turnover was very high (both cause and effect!). I had no time scale, no detail, just a deep inner conviction that it was possible, and would be achieved, and that it would be achieved by setting more specific goals within that vision. The overriding vision was one that no one could take from me, and one which I could share because it was part of my very being.

I had absolute faith in its being achieved. A favourite memory is the sharing of this vision with someone applying to be a manager. He had been offered a higher salary elsewhere in the city, but he was more attracted by the vision that was shared. The joint enthusiasm inspired others. We did it.

Our present vision, one in which we can all share, is the unlocking of our potential! Believe it can be done. Hold on to it! Love it!

The more powerful is that vision in your heart the more powerfully does the law of attraction share it out with your colleagues. And an interesting side benefit is that if things do go wrong, there will be a forgiveness because the motive is clear, a redoubling of effort, because the overall objective, the clarity of vision, is not shaken. Vision and patience work hand in hand.

4) Vigilance

This is an uncommon word, but vital none the less. A good definition is **"watchful attention"**. So much of what we have looked at so far is dependent upon the way we watch our thinking. Are our thoughts in line with PERFECT or IMPERFECT models, how quickly do we see the unwanted thought coming and reject it before it takes hold? We should becoming more and more aware of the need for controlling thought not just in broad terms but every single second of the day. There are many expressions and sayings which relate, for example: "Why sink the ship for a ha'pth of tar"; "A stitch in time saves nine". We have the story of Achilles' heel. The little gap in defence, the minor acceptance of a fault, the breach in a dam which becomes a full flood.

Why should we consider that 99% is acceptable when the final 1% is the one that can lead to our destruction! We simply must not let the wedge of discouragement or inaccurate criticism or lack of forgiveness creep in at the 1% hole in our thinking for it to become fatal! The famous story of the little Dutch boy plugging the dam with his finger shows the importance of stopping even the smallest flaw..

There are many, many, examples of people who have suffered tragic loss or torture and who have survived because they were able to control their thought, and forgive. The temptation to seek revenge must have been very great, yet these individuals have been able to give watchful attention to their *every* thought, (and it has needed to be every thought). 100% control. They are models of serenity, courage, wisdom. If they can forgive, shouldn't we find it possible in those lesser situations in which we find ourselves??? Wyndam's book "The Ultimate Freedom" tells of his survival in a Japanese prisoner of war camp, and crucial in that was his determination to "Control Thought", which included forgiveness and indeed, love..

How do we control thought? We start now! We can still just use cold logic. Is it better to have one of our "PERFECT" words in thought, or one of the" IMPERFECT". Choose just one of those "PERFECT" words and let it be in your thought right now! Right now, your thought *is* 100% PERFECT! **If it is possible for a few moments it then becomes possible for a few more.** But for each of us there will be moments, periods, some short some long, where we let the IMPERFECT thoughts loiter and seemingly kill our potential. All we need to do is to practice getting rid of them! There will be times when we do and times when we don't.

Are we to condemn ourselves when we don't? No.

We looked earlier at the need for forgiveness, both forgiving oneself and others. **It is important to recognise that we will make mistakes as we progress.** If we make a mistake all we have to do is to weed it out. **There is no need to hang on to a mistake**, certainly no need to let it grow. Having learnt from it, the mistake has served its temporary purpose, and can be consigned to the dustbin. If we do not learn from our mistakes they will of necessity recur until we do. Why wait?

Let us find joy in the knowledge that if our motive is right, our progress is inevitable. **Accept we will make mistakes, and know we have the power to learn from them as we root them out.** Let's be vigilant in our forgiveness and other qualities we wish to attract into our experience.

5) Objectivity

This is the climb to the third floor of our house, (it's already going well!!), and again we have a most important room to enter and fill. The need for objectivity is seen in **the need to stand back from any situation and assess it on its merits.** Look back to the section on climbing mountains. Indeed one can look again at all the IMPERFECT words we have listed and recognise that *all* of them would defraud our natural sense of justice and ethics, and try to divert us from right action.

I remember listening to Ray Pelletier when we were both doing presentations in Kobe, Japan. He made the point that if you were shopping in a big supermarket and saw something on offer to which you had strong objections, would you decide to abandon your full trolley and leave the shop empty-handed? Most would pass by. Some might also raise an objection with management. In simple terms, **objectivity is getting the right** balance, based on what is known, and what we know to be right..

When we act to the best of our understanding, taking the balance of everything of which we are aware, a course of action will be revealed that follows the logic of what is required. **If our motive is right and truly objective, the laws of Progress, Attraction, and Expectancy will ensure that even if we make a wrong decision, we can expect the right solution to become apparent** in a way which will give us progress not regression.

So much potential is locked up by situations responding to the pull of personality, self justification, self love. These qualities cannot lead to perfect solutions, whereas principle, responsibility, effective communication will point the way. **When making any decision it is important to objectively consider what or who is influencing thought.** If the salesman was not present, the powerful chairman, even the expectations of others, would you decide differently. Ask yourself "What is the right decision based on what I know to be true?" **How can one make a right decision if one's objectivity is clouded?**

Last year I watched a bumble bee that was trapped in our conservatory. It was making no headway, continually buzzing against the clear glass. It kept trying to go forward. I rescued the little creature, and in that rescue it got me thinking, and led me to write the poem in the Appendix "The Bumble Bee", (subsequently read out on Radio Cornwall) When we make no headway, -like being faced with the steep slope of the mountain, we need to just stand back, draw a deep breath, and look at all the options. Sometimes the quiet thought takes away the extraneous, and the right answer is revealed. This then requires access to the next room!

6) Obedience

From whence comes obedience? There is a lovely quote from the Bible: *"And thine ears shall hear a word behind thee, saying, This is the way, walk ye in it, when ye turn to the right hand, and when ye turn to the left."*

We have all experienced in quiet thinking the sense that someone is talking to us. We can't be obedient unless we listen, put aside self-will, and give full attention to what is being said or even just intimated. Love is in listening.

The huge challenge of obedience when other pressures are brought to bear is one that includes the whole spectrum of ethics. The potential complexity of decision can be eased by consideration of the thought "Be true to yourself" **Be obedient to follow those inner most thoughts which tell you that the way you feel, deep down, is the proper way to act.**

Another way to look at the situation is to again refer to the PERFECT model, and ask the question **"Is what I am going to do going to bring me closer or take me further away from the model I wish to be?"** Yet again we see those prayers from the Middle Ages flooding in, serenity to learn from the past, courage to do what is required, wisdom to know what is right.

As a quick aside, let's not make the excuse that wisdom comes from age, and until we are properly mature, we have no access to wisdom. Wisdom is the capacity and understanding to do what is right, and any one at any age can have that perspicacity and insight to determine right action and be obedient to it. The innocent perspective of a childlike thought often cuts through all the paraphernalia of sophisticated argument, and leaves the individual laughing happily with the simplicity of a solution.

Solutions are joyful. They are revelations of the possible, in which we find freedom.

And in the same way that only obedience to the law of mathematics will enable a mathematical solution to be found, obedience to the traffic light sequence gives a flow of traffic, only obedience to what is right enables the discovery of the very best solutions in our lives. More fundamentally, **obedience to what is right leads to the freedom both to do and to be what is right.**

We can again refer to the example of those who have been under great duress. It was their obedience to themselves, the spirit within, that led to their being free from revenge, hostility, rancour, and remorse.

We move onto the last two rooms.

7) Listening

AM I LISTENING OR TELLING?

Which comes first? The temptation is often to tell first, get one's own point across first, then, possibly, listen to the others. There may even be a temptation to feel that the more important we are, the less we have to listen, the more to order other people about. The obedience which comes from responding to instructions given by others has its own importance within the context of a given situation. The obedience we are seeking, as we have seen above, is one that is responsive to the voice within. There is therefore a requirement to LISTEN to what that voice is saying.

Vision can be likened to the seeing of what is possible, while listening relates to the hearing of what is possible. Both require us to be still, to silence the persuasiveness of what the self wants / intends / demands, and to let the underlying reality of what can be truly perceived speak to us or become visible in its own way. **The less we seek to impress, the more we find we express.** If we are impressing, we are listening to ourselves telling us how grand we are. Our motives are inward. As we learn to listen we in effect tune ourselves in to the radio waves of our true potential which cover every wave band over an infinite frequency.

Effective listening means giving of one's self 100% to the other person or indeed to the stillness of infinity. In this listening mode, one reaches beyond the surface impressions to what has been called in management training "listening to the music" - the underlying communication, the unspoken word or message that enables one to respond to the deeper needs, to reach the requisites of reality. We unlock potential because we are responding to latent potential. We cannot truly respond until we have listened. **A favourite saying taken on board this last year has been "LISTEN, THEN RESPOND WITH LOVE".** It's made me far more aware of how easy is to talk first and not be able to get the right balance / objectivity in what one is saying. Humility helps.

8) Leadership

This may at first sight appear a strange requirement in this last room, but it is a most important one. It is almost a consequence of all the other attributes. Follow the other seven paths, which are not too dissimilar to the noble paths of the Buddhist, the straight and narrow way of the Christian, and leadership qualities will be evident to a high order.

One of the key themes of Unlocking Potential is that we unlock our potential as we unlock the potential of others. **EVERY THOUGHT WE HAVE LOCKS OR UNLOCKS TO A DEGREE THE POTENTIAL OF EVERYBODY ELSE.**

The balance of our thinking weighs in the balance of world thought, and either adds or detracts from the overall balance, the overall tendency, for good or bad.

The law of attraction will bring into our lives the thoughts we are thinking. We have seen how the PERFECT model is constructive, solution based, unselfish, and needs to be nurtured. This is the requirement of leadership for which we are all responsible. A good leader nurtures the team.

We also have the responsibility to nurture the world! It is simply no good to condemn the violence in the world if we have violence in our thinking. It is no good, apart from the sheer hypocrisy!, to condemn the immorality in the world, if we entertain immoral thoughts. It is no good condemning any of the IMPERFECT ways of acting or conducting our lives if we have them in our lives, *and are doing nothing about getting rid of them..*

The leadership required from everyone of us is to behave in the way we wish others to behave, and to set by example the standards by which we wish to live. A good motto from Junior Chamber International is **"THINK GLOBALLY: ACT LOCALLY".** The effect *is* global.

So, we now have our house filled with these eight core qualities, and they are illustrated in the diagram

LISTENING	LEADERSHIP
OBJECTIVITY	OBEDIENCE
VISION	VIGILANCE
ETHICS	EFFORT

Every one of these words can be found in our PERFECT words to which we have been regularly referring. It is simply just the best place to live!

Running through the fabric of this building can be seen the word **LOVE**. And when love is in our heart and our home we also fulfill the saying that "home is the dearest spot on earth"(Eddy). We cannot unlock our potential unless we love our home, and our conscious thoughts

Adherence to these qualities in our thought becomes self fulfilling. "As a man thinketh in his heart so is he", and the 100% filling of consciousness with this way of thinking means that opposite ways of thinking have literally no room to get in.

Our discussed, full potential is at the level of perfection (both as we each may perceive, and as is!), and the 100% consciousness is a reflection of that full potential realised. It may therefore be representative of the mountain top, with ourselves some way below. But the mountain top exists, and others become visible as we reach higher. Our potential exists. And we reach the 100% a step at a time, from where ever we may be on the slopes (or crevice, or base camp).

There may be a number of paths that actually reach the summit of achievement. They all have one thing in common. They all eventually lead upwards. As we fill our thoughts with honest endeavour we can have the certainty that we are progressing in the only direction that is ultimately possible, the way the law of Progress takes us, the way of unlocked potential.

Mountaineers always have a base camp established before they go higher. Let's establish our camp and home with the expectancy of success, and keep it fully stocked with everything we need! In business start-ups, for example, it is axiomatic to consolidate one's position before reaching too far ahead.

Psalm 23 in the Bible is one that many people know, whether Christian or not. It has poetical beauty. It can be seen as a statement of fulfilled potential. What more fitting end could there be to this chapter than the last verse, recognizing as we must that our house is our thinking:

"Surely goodness and mercy shall follow me all the days of my life: and I will dwell in the house of the LORD for ever."

To dwell in a house where love reigns, in particular the qualities earlier described, would be just perfect! Now this expectation should be seen as representing, under the fundamental laws we have discussed, the present actuality of our potential. This is beyond positive thinking and visualisation. It is the realisation of what is already in our house, that these qualities are part of our true being, our true heritage, and as we exercise them we draw closer to their fulfilment in our lives.

WHERE ARE YOU LIVING - EIGHT CORE QUALITIES

SUMMARY

Let's fill our lives with:

LISTENING	LEADERSHIP
OBJECTIVITY	OBEDIENCE
VISION	VIGILANCE
ETHICS	EFFORT

Fill our lives with LOVE, twice over!!

We unlock our potential as we

+ PERCEIVE the above
+ DO the above.
+ LIVE the above.
+ LOVE the above

WHERE WOULD YOU LOVE TO LIVE?

THE GUARANTEE OF SUCCESS

Earlier on in the book we looked at the challenge of using the word "PERFECT". In the previous chapter, we built a mental home, and the first letters of each of the qualities we embedded in our thinking, our mental home, spelled out the word "LOVE".

We need LOVE to be the foundation of our thinking. It is the bedrock which supports everything else. Let us be very clear as to its true nature. The word bedrock is important because it gives the lie to the convenient and throw away remarks that love is like a sponge, and is weak, wishy-washy, namby pamby, call it what derogatory word you will. We have seen in the above statement the focus of love is to reach a goal, and it must be clear to anyone that the achievement of that goal takes determination, courage, perseverance, patience.

Everything we have been discussing comes together in the acceptance of the following sentence, one I have shared with many, paraphrased from Richard Bach's book "Jonathan Livingston Seagull": **"the most important thing in life is to reach out and touch perfection in that which you most love to do..."**

Think of something that you *love* to do. Isn't there a deep desire to do it perfectly well, simply because in doing it "perfectly" it reflects the purest expression of the love that we have towards it. This is the thrill of excellence to which we have already referred, - it is the thrill of watching someone at the pinnacle of their skills in sport, acting, speaking, the beauty and satisfaction of a job well done. In an organizational sense, it is the satisfaction of seeing teamwork produce the result required, when a plan comes to fruition, when all the hours of practice have their fulfillment, **when the technical preparation transcends to the inspirational performance.**

When you love something, there is the **confident expectancy that you will achieve the goal because that is the only way of loving what you are seeking to do.** *Not to achieve your goal is not to love it enough.*

At the start one key objective was to achieve more with less effort, and we have noted that when we give of our love, proportionately less effort is required. We are drawn towards the logical and challenging statement that **as we move towards perfect performance, proportionally less effort is involved.** Practice makes perfect, and performance ultimately becomes instinctive, effort free.

If something is becoming an effort, the self is becoming more important than the object of our attention, in other words, the attention is no longer "perfect"!

Perfect attention, perfect love, takes no effort, *once it has been attained.* That perhaps is the catch, and a very big one. Climbing the mountain may be a route of pain, joy, exhilaration. BUT at the summit, when the goal is reached, at the solution level, the effort is forgotten in the joy of fulfilment. The goal is worth it!! **The self is absent in giving to others, and effort has**

therefore nothing to which it can attach itself. Love unlocks
potential. As referred to in an earlier chapter, it is performance
that takes place "in the zone".

I love dancing. I simply forget myself in the joy of sharing and
dancing with others, immersed in the rhythm of the music.
It becomes effortless. I am sure everyone will have similar
examples where time seems to vanish, - it is the "touching of
perfection in that which you most love to do". Which leads us
nicely this theme:

1. LOVE WHAT YOU DO

If one had a wish, it could be for everybody when they woke up
to be able to say " I'm looking forward to the rest of the day; I
love what I am going to be doing". Forget just for a moment what
may be your present doubts. If you could start the day genuinely
feeling this way, wouldn't that be something to which one could
and should look forward? Let the day unfold with love at its
helm. For example, in business, if love was felt by every member
of your organisation, wouldn't that be a great place to work?! Yet
how many of us still feel envious of those who love their jobs!
How often have your heard or said: "Aren't they lucky, having
a job they love!"

IT IS YOUR DECISION WHETHER YOU LOVE YOUR JOB OR NOT!

BUT how can I love my job when it is full of all those
IMPERFECT words? We have to rely on the fundamental
laws which unlock potential helping us. Value yourself, seek
those elements out in which you excel, let those elements be
projected by and attracted to you, see them in the work you are
doing, and they will become more evident in your experience.

Make the opportunities to demonstrate your self worth in what you do, and make your job, and what you do, an expression of what you truly are. **The Law of Progress will ensure that you are in the right job at the right time, and that you will find the right job, whether you have one now or need to change.**

In the changes in employment I experienced, each of which led to significant progression, the openings became available when I established true motives, - not having to work, but wanting to contribute as much as possible. I found daily employment in expressing those qualities I wished to see in my future employer's *modus operandi*, and what I wanted them to see in me. The laws of self worth, attraction, and expectancy guaranteed I would find employment, and the right work was obtained in its own right time.

It is surely axiomatic that if we are seeking to be employed, obtain contractual work, or take on staff, we will attract what we project. If we can love what we do, there is an underlying enthusiasm which sets one apart from many other people. Who would you rather employ or be with? The person who is in the job for their own benefit alone, or the person who genuinely loves what they are doing, seeking excellence not just for themselves but for the organisation as a whole? Who is going to be more supportive, more alert to opportunities, more employable, more able to unlock the wider potential of every person with whom they make contact?

Do these other people therefore lack potential? No. They are further away from using the potential they have, and it is commercial realism to take on those individuals who are more willing to give of themselves, and have shown that willingness in the past. If you love what you do, the willingness is always there.

My objective when employing staff was to find those who did not have to come to work, not just want to come to work, but would love to come to work. Enthusiasm and experience were sometimes more important than technical qualification.

The above paragraphs have focused on employment. If we widen the comments again to that sense of being employed doing those things which demonstrate our true worth, it becomes apparent that whatever we are doing, there is a joy in doing so with love, and the joy increases as we inevitably do it better. As a general rule, anyone performing with love in their heart (and often therefore with a smile on their face), will be performing at a higher and more successful level.

2. LOVE WHAT YOU ARE

The whole essence of self worth is brought into focus by the need to perceive and understand that what we truly are is unique and worth loving! Our final statement in the law of self worth is that we are what we truly are, and we have already seen that no one can take that away from us. Our potential cannot change. It is inherent and unique in each one of us, and as we turn to the PERFECT words, (acknowledging that there are many many others), *that* is what we love in ourselves *and in others.*

When the tramp looked at the violin he saw a musical instrument which had within it the potential to express music. An obvious comment. When we look at ourselves or at one another, how much of the potential do we really, truly, *see?* The potential to be what we are? To express in manhood / womanhood the full potential of MAN?

I want to be me because within my potential is all I could ever want to be. The team in which I work, the organisation for which I work, is unique, because it is comprised of individuals who are themselves unique. Everybody is of vital importance simply because without them the "sphere" in which they move would be unable to express its full potential without their contribution.

If an orchestra was required to play a composition "perfectly", it would be necessary for every single note of every single instrument to be played perfectly. Who then is more important in the performance of perfection, the pianist who may play thousands of notes, or the individual who may have to play just one note on the triangle? **Everyone is always important.** How frustrating it would be if a stringed instrument could successfully visualise it being a woodwind! As we have seen that is not the way to go or to be.

If we can accept that it is a valid goal to seek perfection, to seek the perfect balance, to be part of the perfect performance of life, to move towards unlocking the full potential that we have, each one of us is special in that context, because without each person's contribution the goal cannot be reached. How important then to value one another, and to recognise the potential that we have.

Not just recognise that potential. But to love that potential. To give it perfect attention. We become what we think about. Our perceptions necessarily move into line with reality. **We can love the perfect model that we hold in thought because the perfect model is the reality of our potential, the capacity to perform perfectly.**

Who can be perfect? Isn't it plain common sense that we have "warts and all", and to seek to be perfect is dangerous? It all depends upon what we are looking at! Our true self worth transcends the physical outreach. The PERFECT words have no boundaries. Our potential has no boundaries.

We move on from the visualization thought "I feel fantastic" to the more accurate "I *am* fantastic". **I am what my potential is.** And therefore this bold statement that each one of us can say, *understanding* why we can say it, **I LOVE WHAT I AM.**

This is the reason we can also turn to every person we meet and think quietly and confidently " I LOVE WHAT YOU ARE", *perceiving* **the reality of** *their* **potential. We unlock (perceive) our potential as we unlock (perceive) the potential of others.**

An effective start to the day is for the first thought to be "I love what I am", and "I love what you are", thinking of one's family, and of the world. **This is the reason we can look at our business, organization and love what it stands for.**

This perception becomes our vision of what is true, and as we actually perceive it and focus on it, that vision becomes true in our experience. If we cannot see the vision, the law of expectancy is still fulfilled: "I knew it was not possible".

Let's move on to one more example. Many of you will know of the intriguing books and pictures called Magic Eye. They are, on the surface, simply coloured designs which look pretty, but have no form. However, as one looks at them carefully, after a time of focusing the eyes at different levels, a picture suddenly appears in full 3D. It is literally a magic moment. It would appear that some people are unable to see these pictures. Others can. For those that cannot, for whatever reason, (and for *some* it is simply not giving sufficient attention), it doesn't mean that the 3D image is not there. It simply has not been seen.

Our potential, what we truly are, is like this magic eye. It takes an effort to see it, but once seen it's never forgotten. **Our potential is too vast to visualise, but not too vast to love.** I love what I am: I love what you are....

We have considered the value of humility, the stillness of thought that reaches out to the universe and places oneself in the grandeur of Creation. For millions of people their concept of Divinity includes the all-embracing prayer of "Our Father", - a recognition that man is the creation of God, and that is what we truly are. To start the morning with the affirmation "God made me!" is self-worth, attraction and expectancy in three simple words!

Finally, **the most effective way to love what you are is to do those things which express what you truly are.** The catch, then, if there is one, or rather the blunt realism which needs to be applied to make this practical and not esoterical, is that **the *only* way to truly love what you are, is to *be* what you are.**

3. BE WHAT YOU ARE

Herein is the clash between the theoretical and the practical. It is no good claiming to be "PERFECT" when one's actions are "IMPERFECT". Who then can ever claim to be perfect? For many the acceptance of faults is an important comfort, -"take me as I am". If our potential is perfection, whenever and if ever that may be realised, don't we bring its realisation nearer by having the perfect model in thought and doing those things which the perfect model would be doing? Rather than each day condemning ourselves for failing to live up to the perfect model, can't we rather rejoice that each day we are nearer understanding and demonstrating it? Constant condemnation is going to attract the wrong thoughts, and lead in the wrong direction.

If our motive is to be what we are, that **motive sets the direction in which we walk,** and by the law of expectancy and attraction to that goal, **we are drawn inevitably towards the fulfilment of self worth, to being what we truly are.**

The common sense and logic of *being / expressing* what we truly are is inescapable. Our true self *is* happy: *be* happy. Whether through prayer, meditation, or however we wish to give quiet thought, be still, and *feel* whatever is our true being. One of my favourite Bible verses is "Be still, and know that I am God". In that stillness, we can all recognise that we are something special. And in gratitude, be that someone special. There is no other way!

If you want to fulfil your potential, *be* that potential as far as you can perceive it, express it in every thing you do.

This takes love, and vision, and vigilance, and practice. There are no short cuts, and one can start or continue from here and now.

We are responsible for managing our lives.

There is no stress in love, because love is not something one can force.

Love just *is.*

Ralph Waldo Emmerson said that what lies behind us and what

lies before us are but tiny matters compared to what lies within us. Love lies within us. It is the essence of our potential

Our potential is not something which changes.

It is. It exists. It is what we are and wherever we are.

If we can relax into being what we are there is no stress or tension, because we are aligning ourselves with what is. **The law of attraction holds us by the hand and takes us, individually, towards the inevitable expression of what we truly are.**

We can therefore relax, confident that these laws operate in our lives, and universally.

Perceive what you are, focus on the existence of these laws, be at one with them, and be the potential that you are.

The chapter heading was to give the guarantee of success. The self fulfilling guarantee is "Be successful", let your thinking be aligned to success, rooting out all thoughts of failure. Each apparent failure must be seen as a stepping stone to a different solution to the one we first envisaged. Each failure is a step nearer success. Failure only happens when you stop trying.

Failure also only happens when you stop loving, for the motivation of love is surely to succeed, to keep trying, because the goal is always in thought, and some other way always presenting itself.

Eddy writes "Love inspires, illumines, designates and leads the way. Right motives give pinions to thoughts and strength and freedom to speech and action". I have shared this at many meetings. There is no denying its veracity and power. No denying its truth. Who hasn't proved it in their own experience?

Living these core qualities is living in love. How's that for a vision of what you take with you, as an individual or organisation!

Let me quote from a dear friend, Ray Seddon. We had been discussing the workshop, and he wrote this to me in a letter back in the 1990's, - well before its time!! It is a good way to end this chapter.

The Importance of Love

"Love unifies, heals broken relationships, dissolves barriers. overcomes fears and resentment.

It is the lubricating oil of any organisation, enabling its parts to work together with maximum effectiveness and minimum friction.

Love promotes co-operation, sharing, mutual support. It opens our eyes to new possibilities, enlightening consciousness as sunshine brightens the landscape.

It constitutes a work environment or atmosphere of thought in which people feel free to be themselves, to express their innate creativity and take fresh, mould breaking initiatives uninhibited by fear of criticism.

What a difference there is between working in an atmosphere of mutual respect and appreciation and one where back biting, rivalry, and conflict occurs between individuals and departments. Which is likely to be the happy one, the efficient one, the progressive one?

Love brings joy and fulfillment in one's work and this job satisfaction has its effect on the health of both the employee and the business.

Love gives an inner strength to individuals and organizations to meet the tough challenges and "thousand natural shocks that flesh is heir to"- Hamlet.

To live in accord with the inner motivation of love lifts the individual above the chore of merely complying with imposed external demands and confers a freedom obtainable in no other way.

To put it briefly, love brings out the best in people and the organisations for which they work."   *Ray Seddon*

THE GUARANTEE OF SUCCESS

SUMMARY

- ✦ LOVE WHAT YOU DO

- ✦ LOVE WHAT YOU ARE

- ✦ BE WHAT YOU ARE

- ✦ KEEP LOVING!

The most important thing in life is to reach out and touch perfection in what you most love to do.

TOWARDS EFFECTIVE ACTION!

The Unlocking Potential workshops which have formed the practical basis for this book were successful because they followed and proved the ideas as laid out. Goals that people had not dared to believe become tangible, shared, and once fully perceived and discussed, came the realisation that they were indeed obtainable. And were so proved.

One of the joys of both the effective speaking course and the unlocking potential seminars was the teamwork that developed, - the building of sometimes unexpected trust, - the recognition of achievement, a new self belief that each could share. What propelled the further success of all these individuals? A fundamental requirement for all progress is that mixture of praise and gratitude that recognises a job well done, - a good motive blessed for its application. How a child reacts with joy to the loving encouragement of its parents, even when things do not go as planned. And how often do we discourage by focusing on the small failures when much more has been achieved than we recognise.

Love by its nature is something that encourages . Eddy writes "Love is reflected in love", - it is the natural response that underlies all the potential that is ours to demonstrate, the underlying wish to please that is inherent in us all.

THE IMPACT OF LOVE

Across both Eastern and Western philosophies and religions, there is a simple yet profound statement that bears repeating and thinking through. The purpose of love is to express itself. And there are millions of people across the world who are quietly reaching out and changing lives because love is doing what it does, with humility and untold power. Like the tramp and the violin, we will never know how far our good actions touch the hearts of others and springboard their lives. We all have that potential..

Whoever will just stand back, and look at the life of Jesus, and what impact this man has had on history and on present lives, will see what potential is possible. Jesus saw his source as God, he saw all of us as sons and daughters of God (Our Father...). He overcame material laws, healed, inspired, overcame everything thrust at him, and promised we could do more!

Jesus was motivated by love, and that motivation flowed through his disciples then and through history. For nearly all religious denominations the words of John ring true: "God is love; and he that dwelleth in love dwelleth in God and God in him". Imagine the power that is thus represented when we let whatever concept we have of God rule our lives. Others too, throughout history, have given of themselves that deep yearning to love one another, and in so doing have surpassed what normal is, to reach the acme of brotherhood. When we love what we do, what we are, we reach into a level of thought that enables us to reach towards perfection. We all have examples, sometimes hidden away, that we can realise that what we have achieved might have been thought impossible. These are but glimpses of the reality that one example proves the whole. 2+2=4 opens up the universe of mathematics. Love your neighbor as yourself opens up the universe of perfect achievement. It has been proved. It has been witnessed.

When we align ourselves to the true nature of love we align ourselves to the most powerful intelligence and force in the universe. As already indicated, for the religious, this is clearly aligning themselves with God. The following poem shares my personal vision:

LOVE IS EVERYTHING

O Lord my God let love for Thee
Take over all my being,
Let recognition of true self
Just flood through all I'm seeing.

In gratitude for God's great Love
I find my life in You.
And thus I find Your Love o'erflows,
In everything I do.

On a general level, this poem reflects a desire to be fully with one's own recognition of their true source of being, to establish true self worth, to let love be what motivates and unlocks potential.

It brings to mind one of the most powerful verses in the whole of the Bible, that stands as another universal maxim: "ye shall know the truth, and the truth shall make you free". This begs two questions, - what is the truth, and free from what? We have looked at what is reality / truth. It is your true being. Freedom is freedom from whatever limits, restricts. It is a call to recognise that our potential truly is unlimited.

Love is the first step, next step, every step. It is what frees us, unites us, lifts us, and gives us all we need. Everyone has proved at some point the power of love in their lives, whether in family, sport, art, business, anything with sharing. Let's enjoy proving it all the time.

Unlock your potential. Be love. Live love.

LET LOVE BE YOUR ALL.

BE FREE.

With love

Ken G Cooper

TOWARDS EFFECTIVE ACTION!

SUMMARY

- POTENTIAL IS THE FULFILLMENT OF LOVE.
- LOVE YOURSELF FOR WHAT YOU TRULY ARE.
- LOVE YOUR NEIGHBOR AS YOURSELF.
- LOVE IS YOUR TRUE POTENTIAL.

LET LOVE BE YOUR ALL:

BE FREE!

APPENDICES

CHALLENGING WORDS ARISING FROM WORKSHOPS ON UNLOCKING POTENTIAL

A PRACTICAL EXERCISE

*These **PERFECT** words represent your true qualities; they give solutions.*

Nurture these seeds

Professional	Positive	Persistent	Practical
Pure	Praising	Principled	Progressive
PERFECT!	Punctual	Precise	Productive
Peaceful	Planning	Prayerful	Perspicacious
Profitable			

Effective	Efficient	Enthusiastic	Enquiring
Empathetic	Energetic		

Responsible	Reasonable	Reliable	Responsive
Recognitive	Ready	Risk accepting	<u>Respect</u>ful
Repentant	Resourceful	Rewarding	

Fearless	Factual	Frank	Friendly
Forgiving	Fun-giving	Failure OK. if practicing for success	
Fair	Flexible	Faithful	Focused
Free	Furthering	Flowing	Family
Excellence	Encouraging	Enduring	**Ethical**
Expectant	Enterprising		
Caring	Communicative	Committed	Confident
Courageous	Creative	Considerate	Controlled
Can Do	Compassionate	Concentrating	Consistent
Trusting	Teamworking	Truthful	Tolerant
Thankful	Thoughtful		

*These **IMPERFECT** words need changing; they lead to problems.*

Root our these weeds by doing their opposite.

Intolerant	Insecure	Insolent	Infatuated
Insincere	Immoral	Inhibited	Insular
Inhospitable	Inactive	Invidious	Introspective
Impressionistic	If-Centred	Imperfect	Intolerant
Mediocre	Mendacious	Minimalist	Motive-Inward
Malicious	Malcontent	Mocking	Materialistic
Mistrustful	Mucky		
Personality	Promiscuous	Procrastinating	Professionalist
Pedantic	Provocative	Pessimistic	Prevaricating
Perfectionist	Petty	Passionate	Proud
(Self)Punishing	Perjuring	Panicking	

Ego-centred	Evil	Excuseful (I'm Just Not Responsible)	
Exaggerating	Excessive		
Ridiculing	Rumour	Resentful	Rancorous
Revengeful	Risk (Unsupported)	Rigid`	
Retrospective	Restrictive	Ruminatingr	Rock-Like
Fearful	Flatterer	Festating	Favour-Seeking
Fashion-Led	Falsifying		
Easeful	Escapist	Evasive	Envious
Emotionalist	Erratic		
Complacent	Calculating	Cowardly	Cheat
Can't	Corrupt	Conflicting	Cop Out
Clever (Sly)	Carefree	Cruel	Callous
Tempted	Treacherous	Threatening	Techniquing
Time-bound	Tyrannical		

WE EXPERIENCE AND PROMOTE WHAT WE ARE THINKING.

Refer to main text pps 46-61. Circle, or just think about, the words that best represent you, your home, workplace, - you choose. Nurture what you're best at, reverse what needs to be changed. It can be done. It has been done.

Unlock Potential-With Love

SELECTED BIBLIOGRAPHY

The Bible (primarily KJV, but see The Bible Gateway.com for alternative translations)

Bach, Richard	Jonathan Livingston Seagull
Back, Ken and Kate	Assertiveness at Work
Black, Roger	Getting things Done
Blanchard & Johnson	The One Minute Manager
Clifton, Donald; Nelson, Paula	Play to Your Strengths
Crainer, Stuart	The Ultimate Business Library
Davidow, William; Uttal, Bro	Total Customer Service
Drucker, Peter F	The Frontiers of Management
Eddy, Mary Baker	Science and Health, with key to the Scriptures
Harvey-Jones, Sir John	Making It Happen
Handy, Charles	The search for meaning
Hoyt, Edith Armstrong	Studies in the Apocalypse.
Kidder, Rushworth M	Good People Make Tough Choices
King, Norman	The First Five Minutes
Lovejoy, Surya	Getting Results
McCormack, Mark H	The 110% Solution
Minto, Barbara	The Pyramid Principle
Peel, Robert	Spiritual Healing in a Scientific Age
Peters, Tom	Thriving on Chaos
Peters, Tom; Austin, Nancy	A Passion For Excellence
Robbins, Anthony	Unlimited Power
Thomas, Brian	Total Quality Management.
Various	The Gower Book of Management.
Wyndham, John	The Ultimate Freedom

Upcoming title by Ken G Cooper:
"With Love- a book of Poetry and Prose"

SELECTED POEMS

DIAMOND JUBILEE QUEEN ELIZABETH 1952-2012

Elizabeth Regina, our true star and guiding light,
Our dearest pure-gold Sovereign, yet such a diamond bright!
Sixty years your kingdom and the Commonwealth you have blessed,
Sixty years of selfless rule, always doing what is best.

A beacon to your family, a mother to the state,
You are what makes our country not just good but also great,
Your marriage to Prince Phillip an example to us all,
His constant strong support to you has been an unbreached wall.

He was your childhood sweetheart, you married at twenty one,
But only after five more years the death of Dad did stun.
With duties new and thrust upon our young and married queen
Your coronation televised was by its millions seen.

So Charles and Anne your children grew up with The Queen as mum,
And their childhood was a challenge, for in public it was run.
Yet from that time to both of them their duties were made clear,
Subserving self, the nation first, the Queen's example dear.

Love gave birth to two more sons, Andrew and Edward as well,
And family life at various times gave challenges from hell!
Yet through the pain there was your love that underwrote the whole,
And you have earned such blessings that enrich and mould the soul!

Oh what a beacon you have been to us with problems dire,
The loss of your Britannia and Windsor swept by fire:
These sixty years you've seen enough to make most people weep
And through it all, our dearest Queen, your dignity did keep.

And now we see your children as the finest family tree,
And you and us can sense in them continued history.
And notwithstanding problems let's do get the balance right,
Your love for them and us for you is Britain's beacon bright.

And in that time oh just lets think of all those you have greeted,
Not just the leaders of the world, but public, stood and seated!
Your wisdom and good humour they are second, yea, to none;
When you smile all peoples smile, for you're loved by everyone.

We love you for your honesty, always doing what is true,
We love you for your kindness that just shines through and through:
And when all else is changing, politicians come and go,
Our Christian Queen holds us quite firm, and we have still our Throne.

So on this Diamond Jubilee, some pageant there will be,
And it is in your honour so that all the earth will see!
We love you Queen Elizabeth, and long may you still reign,
And in the history of our world this diamond will remain.

THE GARDENER

The garden was her life. The unfolding seasons as reflected in the changing patterns of what grew and died and returned newborn seemed to her the unfolding of her inner being, parts no longer needed now discarded as outgrown, ever developing in all its glory and becoming ever more stunning in her mind's eye. Each day she would tend some new area, revisit an old; there was never any pattern, but simply as her gaze rested and impulse took her, perhaps as guided by some unseen Hand.

With care and love she nurtured plant, earth, cleared stone wall, removed weeds, seeded, planted, all cleansing and nourishing her soul.

And as the garden grew more beautiful, so did she........

THE BUMBLE BEE

From the unrestricted freedom of the open air,
The bumble bee flew unwittingly into our conservatory.
Within seconds it had bumped and buzzed against an invisible window,
And it repeated its actions in bewildered puzzlement.
Again and again, in futile frustration, the bumping and buzzing
    reverberated.
It just didn't know what was preventing it flying forwards.
So it buzzed and bumped in blind repetition, for that was all it could
    conceive.
Ever more tired and confused, its efforts became more sporadic.
It fell onto the sill, near to giving up,
Gathering strength for a final fling of desperate helpless hope.

It didn't know that its plight had already been heard:
Two kindly hands with glass tumbler and stiff card were on their way.
Sudden entrapment caught the bumble unawares.
In furious fear and tight enclosure, its bewilderment was complete,
It buzzed ferociously, loudly, fighting in utter ignorance of what was
    happening:
But by the open patio door, released and now unfettered, it flew, flew
    skywards!
Zigzagging in the unexpected joy and relief of freedom,
Not knowing how, but wonderfully, gloriously, free.
Free to be itself.

It made me think.
How often do I keep bumping along, seeing no progress, refusing to
    change my ways.
Not realising what was preventing my going forward,
Not knowing what to do, where to go, how to go, so just keeping safe
    (?) in the old routines.
Perhaps puzzled by the world's illogicality,
Not prepared or even too scared, to challenge, or to follow a
    different way,
That is already waiting:

Not realising that sometimes the only way forward is to stop.............
Think. Repent. Be brave enough and wise enough, to do something
     differently.
The bumble bee had been trying too hard. Ultimately, by itself, it
     could do nothing.*
If only it knew that help was at hand.
If only I knew.

Jesus said *"Repent: for the kingdom of heaven is at hand."*

Stop fighting! Yield the mortal self, the arrogance of self-will and
     selfish pride!
The blind and stubborn mortal personality, shouting to exist, must
     go and be no more.
Right where I am, the door to the kingdom is already open, but in
     the other direction!
Love is here, always here, omnipotent hands outstretched in
     tenderness and healing.
Be still... Trust.... Yield..... Let...... Now!
Know and feel that I am, and simply be, God's child.**
For when I knew it not, Love had already taken me up,
Already knew and knows my freedom.

Even in the depths of despair, we can, in sweet self-surrender, suddenly find,
In Love's care and protection, we are already in the heavenly kingdom.
Because Love loves and liberates, releases from all shackles,
We have the absolute freedom of spiritual being:
Wonderfully, gloriously, free.
If only we would turn:
Humble,
Be.

"I can of mine own self do nothing:" John 5:30 (to:)
"Repent: for the kingdom of heaven is at hand." Matt.4:17 Repent
**"Behold, now are we the sons of God" 1 John 3:2 (to 2ⁿᵈ,)*

"I HAVE SET BEFORE THEE AN OPEN DOOR, AND NO MAN CAN SHUT IT" REV.3:18

My life it seemed hemmed in, with walls on every side,
Whichever way I looked, however hard I tried,
Wasn't any future, just how to be set free?
The walls were like a tomb, this not a place to be!

I prayed my heart to God, to show me what to do,
And heard His message clear, "My Love is great for you,
Behold right now, and know, no matter what's been done,
I am your Father-Mother, and love you as My son.

By My very nature, my arms are always wide,
My door is always open, from Love one cannot hide".
I listened and obeyed. One step to Him I trod,
My true home found at last. My life at one with God.

That one step took trust, -and I had to hold God's hand, -
He led me to His kingdom, into the Promised Land!
God's Love was there, 'twas all around, freedom it was won.
I felt and knew a truth divine: I stood as God's own son!

No matter where you are, just one stride lets you in.
Her Love is always there, and takes away all sin.
God can never shutter His constant love for man,
His door is always open. Walk right through now! You can!

MOTIVATIONAL BIBLE QUOTES
(Taken from the King James Version 1611 AD)

Was the Bible one of the first management handbooks ever written? Irrespective of your faith or beliefs, read these motivational quotes and be inspired.

Gen. 1:27 1ˢᵗ God
God created man in his *own* image, in the image of God created he him; male and female created he them.

Gen. 1:31 (to 1ˢᵗ .)
And God saw every thing that he had made, and, behold, *it was* very good.

Lev. 19:18 2ⁿᵈ thou
thou shalt love thy neighbour as thyself: I *am* the Lᴏʀᴅ.

Eccl. 3:1, 14 (to 2ⁿᵈ :)
To every *thing there is* a season, and a time to every purpose under the heaven:
I know that, whatsoever God doeth, it shall be for ever: nothing can be put to it, nor anything taken from it:

Psalms 23:6
Surely goodness and mercy shall follow me all the days of my Life: and I will dwell in the house of the Lord for ever.

Psalms 143:10
Teach me to do thy will; for thou art my God: thy spirit is good; lead me in unto the land of uprightness.

Prov. 3:13, 14
Happy *is* the man *that* findeth wisdom, and the man *that* getteth

understanding. For the merchandise of it *is* better than the merchandise of silver, and the gain thereof than fine gold.

Prov. 4: 23, 26
Keep thy heart with all diligence; for out of it are the issues of life.
Ponder the path of thy feet, and let all thy ways be established.

Prov. 8:17
I love them that love me; and those that seek me early shall find me.

Prov. 23:7 as (to :)
as he thinketh in his heart, so *is* he:

Prov. 24:14 2ⁿᵈ thy
thy expectation shall not be cut off.

Isa. 30:21
And thine ears shall hear a word behind thee, saying, This is the way, walk ye in it, when ye turn to the right hand, and when ye turn to the left.

Matt. 5 :48
Be ye therefore perfect, even as your Father in heaven is perfect.

Matt. 6:8 for, 12 1ˢᵗ forgive, 21, 22, 33 seek
for your Father knoweth what things ye have need of, before ye ask him.
forgive us our debts, as we forgive our debtors.
For where your treasure is, there will your heart be also.
The light of the body is the eye: if therefore thine eye be single, thy whole body shall be full of light.
seek ye first the kingdom of God, and his righteousness; and all these things shall be added unto you.

Matt. 7:7
Ask, and it shall be given you; seek, and ye shall find; knock, and it shall be opened unto you:

Mark 11:24 What
What things soever ye desire, when ye pray, believe that ye receive *them*, and ye shall have *them*.

Luke 17:21 behold
behold, the kingdom of God is within you.

John 5:19
Then answered Jesus and said unto them, Verily, verily, I say unto you, The Son can do nothing of himself, but what he seeth the Father do: for what things soever he doeth, these also doeth the Son likewise.

John 14:12
Verily, verily, I say unto you, He that believeth on me, the works that I do shall he do also; and greater *works* than these shall he do; because I go unto my Father.

Acts 17:27 1ˢᵗ they, 28 (to ;)
they should seek the Lord, if haply they might feel after him, and find him, though he be not far from every one of us: For in him we live, and move, and have our being;

Rom. 13:8, 10
Owe no man any thing, but to love one another: for he that loveth another hath fulfilled the law.

Gal. 6:7 for
for whatsoever a man soweth, that shall he also reap.

Phil. 4:13
I can do all things through Christ which strengtheneth me.

James 1:4 let, 8
let patience have *her* perfect work, that ye may be perfect and entire, wanting nothing.
A double-minded man *is* unstable in all his ways.

James 3:11, 12
Doth a fountain send forth at the same place sweet *water* and bitter? Can the fig tree, my brethren, bear olive berries? either a vine, figs? so *can* no fountain both yield salt water and fresh.

I John 3:2 (to 2ⁿᵈ,)
Beloved, now are we the sons of God,

I John 4:16 2ⁿᵈ God, 18 1ˢᵗ perfect (to :)
God is love; and he that dwelleth in love dwelleth in God, and God in him.
Perfect love casteth out fear:

IN SUMMARY:

John 8:32 ye
ye shall know the truth, and the truth shall make you free.